AN INTRODUCTORY GUIDE TO SPIRITUAL MATURITY

AN INTRODUCTORY GUIDE TO SPIRITUAL MATURITY

FATHER TOM HERON

Copyright © 2021 by Father Tom Heron

ISBN 978-1-7364750-0-3

All Rights Reserved, including the right to reproduce this book or portions thereof in any form whatsoever. This work is copyrighted by the publisher. No unauthorized duplication or presentation allowed. Reviewers may quote small portions for the sake of review written for inclusion in a magazine, newspaper, or journal; however, expressed, written permission by the publisher is required prior to publication.

For information about special discounts for bulk purchases, please contact the publisher at eleven24sales@gmail.com

Version 1

Because of the dynamic nature of the internet, any web addresses or links contained in this book may have changed since the publication and may no longer be valid.

All names, images, and/or likenesses contained herein have given verbal and/or written permission to the author to be included. Some names have been changed or omitted to protect the privacy of the individuals.

All biblical citations included in this work have been sourced from the New American Bible (Revised Edition), also known as NABRE, unless otherwise noted in the text.

IN THANKSGIVING FOR THE
SIGNIFICANT SPIRITUAL
GUIDES IN MY LIFE

Daniel Murray
William McNamara
Robert Morneau
Sara Lessard
Mary K. McKenna
Jim Meehan
Joe Meehan
Fran Meehan
Bill Mattia
Dot Heron (mother)
John Heron (grandfather)
Jack Heron (for four and a half years until his untimely death at thirty-three years old)
Patrick Kelley
John Lewis
Karen Purcell
Joe Corley
The many children of the church, especially Nora Lynch. Their wonder guides me to be more playful and prayerful in my spiritual journey

CONTENTS

Foreword by Sara Lessard	ix
Preface	xi
Introduction	xv

PART I
THE ADVENT SEASON

1. Joy	5
2. Silence	9
3. Anticipation	11
4. Stillness	15

PART II
THE CHRISTMAS SEASON

5. Childlike Wonder	23
6. Innocence	27
7. Simplicity	31

PART III
THE LENTEN SEASON

8. Suffering Love	39
9. Reconciliation	43
10. False Self vs. True Self	47
11. Conversion	51
12. Discipleship	55

PART IV
THE EASTER SEASON

13. Discernment	63
14. Humility	67
15. Hilarity	71
16. Hospitality	73
17. Holiness	77
18. New Life	81

PART V
THE THREE GREAT FEASTS

19. Identity — 89
20. Intimacy — 95
21. Integrity — 99
22. Leisure — 101

PART VI
ORDINARY TIME

23. Attentive — 109
24. Intelligent — 113
25. Reasonable — 117
26. Responsible — 119
27. Mysticism — 123

Afterword — 127
Acknowledgments — 133
About the Author — 135
Works Cited — 137

FOREWORD

BY SARA LESSARD

Using the liturgical seasons of the church to express and explore core values, Father Tom Heron invites us to reach down to examine our motivations and to reach up to grasp the outstretched hand of Jesus—to discover the rhythm of a personal relationship with Father, Son, and Holy Spirit in whose image we have identity.

With the accuracy and precision of the skilled athlete he is, Father Tom directs our attention toward something we can do, toward a goal we can achieve: spiritual maturity. Thirty years of deep and abiding friendship have led me to know without question that for Father Tom, the altar is a symbol of the banquet table and the divine hospitality to which all are invited.

Father Tom's style is colloquial and approachable. Prayer, study, and his relentless pursuit of the good, the true, and the beautiful that is for God have fashioned for the reader, a worthy guide.

"Where charity and love prevail, there is God." This Holy Thursday antiphon forms the template of this inspiring book. Its chapter headings read like lamp posts directing our attention to issues of personhood and personality. They command attention and provide counsel that instruct and assist us to grow toward integration.

An Introductory Guide to Spiritual Maturity is the thoughtful distillation of a serious disciple. As such, it is as demanding and rigorous as most disciplines we might embrace in our quest for every deepening growth. However, Father Tom's proclivity to tell stories, an inherited Irish trait, his penchant to laugh (often at himself), and his earnestness to engage the reader for the sake of his or her own good, enlivens the spirit and calls us to reach further than we thought possible.

Quickly we find ourselves journeying together, fueled by his conviction and encouraged by an inexhaustible supply of practical and spiritual support. Be prepared to work, but also to wonder at the closeness of God to our own lives, to become friends with the Lord of our longing.

"When we stand before the judgment seat of Christ," says Bishop Robert Barron in a recent YouTube homily, "He will ask whether we have taught the world how to praise, how to reverence the truth, how to go out vigorously on campaign to extend the kingdom of God."

Father Tom has amply equipped us with what is required for us to face that moment unafraid.

PREFACE
CARS, CASH, AND CLOTHES COUNT FOR NOTHING

As I pondered my call to writing yet another book on my vocation, wondering what I could possibly put together after having just published a 350-page chronicle the previous year, I was left thinking about the thoughts, the problems, and the crises we wrestle on a daily basis. It's true, in this day and age, that our sense of the presence of Father, Son, and Holy Spirit is in inverse proportion to the pace of our lives. The enormous increase in the speed of daily life is clearly pathogenic. We live in a nanosecond culture; wheezing and worn out. The entire world seems plagued by this hurry sickness. Virtually all of our relationships are damaged by hurry. We walk fast, talk fast, eat fast, and then announce, "Sorry, I've got to run!"

Jesus would tell us this is no way to live. Remember, He came so that we so that we may have life and have it more abundantly, as He proclaims in John 10:10.

Carl Jung talks about the two halves of life. We establish our identities in the first half. Power, money, success, and celebrity play an inordinate influence in the early stages of life primarily due to a lack of experience.

In his memoir, *Report to Greco*, Nikos Kazantzakis shares

the story of a summer he spent in a monastery. While there, he asked an old monk "Do you still wrestle with the devil, Father Makarios?" The old monk responded, "Not any longer, my child. I have grown old now, and he has grown old with me. He doesn't have the strength....I wrestle with God."[1]

Fr. Ron Rolheiser, a Catholic author and public speaker, reflected upon this story on his blog in 2007, postulating the idea of wrestling with God "suggests that the struggles in later life can be very different than what we struggle with earlier on."[2] That, when we switch our focus from those material things, we begin to struggle with anger and forgiveness—"and that anger is often, however unconsciously, focused on God. In the end, our real struggle is with God," as He challenges us to grow in spiritual maturity and personal holiness.

Wrestling with the ego spirit is always an issue between good and evil. If we allow our ego spirits free reign, we are likely to hurt both others and ourselves. When we enter our mid-30s or even mid-40s, we are challenged to finally establish ourselves. In the best-case scenario, we realize **cars, cash, and clothes count for nothing** in the grand scheme of Gospel living.

If we break through the temptations of power, promiscuity, money, and fame, then compassion, simplicity, and serenity are the new reigns we embrace. We are called to be disciples—to die to selfishness, die to the ego spirit, and die to all things.

The Gospel says to give everything to the poor and follow the way of the Messiah. Yet, "When the young man heard this statement, he went away sad, for he had many possessions." (Matthew 19:22). He wasn't ready. The attachment to material comfort and material possessions is going to be as tenacious a wrestling match with God as it was wrestling with the Evil One to obtain those things in the first place.

If cars, cash, and clothes count for nothing, then what

really counts is a deep, meaningful relationship with Father, Son, and Holy Spirit and with your neighbors so we can give of ourselves and not feel diminished by doing so? The answer is the feeling of enrichment through giving to our children, grandchildren, spouses, and friends. That takes some maturity and that's what I decided this book would be about: **spiritual maturity**.

A simple consent to God's will is that we don't invest ourselves in the relationship at all. We give lip service a tip of the hat—lukewarmness. We try to do God's will out of fear or obedience. However, a mature acquiescence to God's will is that we will work this out together so we may discover what God has called each of us to be.

We've begun to set our sights on spiritual maturity when we accept the challenge of the Gospel. The Gospel is not easy to trust. We must believe His way is better than our way, and we must no longer be motivated by fear and obedience, but a deep understanding rooted in a personal, passionate, and profound relationship with the Risen Lord.

Spiritual maturity is no walk in the park. We cannot go at it alone. That's why I recommend enlisting the guidance of a spiritual director. Protect and be attentive to your spiritual growth as if it were your own child, because as the prophet Isaiah predicted, "The calf and the young lion shall browse together, with a little child to guide them." (Isaiah 11:6).

INTRODUCTION

"I tell you, unless your righteousness surpasses that of the scribes and Pharisees, you will not enter into the kingdom of heaven." (Matthew 5:20)

Jesus tells us we must be holier than the Scribes and Pharisees, who are good, law-abiding people, but have spiritual blind spots, namely hypocrisy and fraud. That word, "righteousness," comes from the Greek "αγιότητα." Other acceptable translations of the word are: holiness, virtue, sainthood or saintliness, and sanctity.[4] However, I've always interpreted this teaching of Jesus as quite literally, "to enter the kingdom of heaven, you must grow in **spiritual maturity**."

The purpose of this handbook is to introduce the reader to the Gospel call to conversion, as well as spiritual growth and maturity. This call is daily and ongoing no matter your age or stage in your life.

A casual reading of the Gospels reveals an unskippable, four-fold pattern of conversion that applies to everyone. Jesus's first words in the Gospel of John are, "What are you looking for?" (John 1:38). These would-be disciples answer a question with a question: "Where are you staying?"

INTRODUCTION

Why did they not answer, "the truth," "inner peace," or "enlightenment"? Jesus appeals to their innate curiosity through invitation:

Come and watch me live life simply and abundantly. Come and listen to my story. Come to an out-of-the-way place and rest with me. Come and learn how to pray. Come and be nourished by me as the bread of life.

After spending some time with Jesus—almost as if it were an apprenticeship—the disciples are prepared for the second step of the conversion process: to be generous. Jesus instructs them:

If someone asks for your shirt, give him or her your cloak, as well. If someone asks you to walk one mile, walk two. The gift you have received, give as gift to others. Oh, and by the way, do not let your left hand know what your right hand is doing.

Do not forget that giving to others can test you, drain you, and maybe even cause you to set strict, rigid limits.

In 1965, I knew of a young man, Joe Corley, a senior at Cardinal Dougherty High School in Philadelphia. After high school, he took courses at the local community college, using public transportation to get there. Every morning, he passed a shoeless, homeless man. Joe was reminded of the Gospel teaching and gave one pair of his own shoes to this man one morning. On the way home, the homeless man stopped Joe and gave the shoes back, because he did not like them. Talk about a true test of your generosity!

After we listen to the Lord and discern how we are being called to be generous in our present life circumstance, then we can prepare ourselves for the third phase of conversion: forgiveness.

As we recite on the Saturday of the first week of Lent, "If

you want to be children of your heavenly Father, then you must pray for those who persecute you and speak all kinds of evil against you."

When we hate our enemies, we give them power over us —power over our sleep, power over our health, power over our peace of mind. They would dance for joy knowing this.

> *"Though one should fall into many and grievous sins and imperfections, he ought never to despair of his salvation nor lose confidence in God, for the Divine clemency is infinitely greater than human malice."*
> *–St. John Chrysostom*[4]

Jesus purposely used wild exaggeration to make an emphatic point when he told the Parable of the Unforgiving Servant in Matthew 18:21-35, telling Peter to forgive seventy-seven times. The world's most miserable person is one who won't forgive. Nothing can gnarl the soul more quickly.

To speak of sin by itself apart from grace is to forget the resolve of divine mercy, but to speak of grace without sin is surely no better. For the disciple of Jesus to ignore, spin, or otherwise mute the reality of sin is to cut the nerve of the Gospel.

> *"As long as you bear your grudge, no matter how 'valid,' there can be no true congregation as far as you are concerned ... Then forgive as much as is in your power and ask God to give you an increase of forgiveness."*
> *–Romano Guardini*[5]

The stage is set for the most difficult step in the conversion process, which is embracing sacrifice and suffering as a necessary part of being a disciple of the Lord. Jesus invites every would-be disciple of His to "take up his cross, and

INTRODUCTION

follow me." (Matthew 16:24). If this were the first step in the conversion process, Jesus would have very few disciples.

We have an instinctive resistance to sacrifice and suffering. Jesus makes a key distinction that is helpful, but still challenging. He tells us to suffer in love—in imitation of him — in order to reduce the suffering in the world that is rooted in sin, hatred, and violence. Love suffering humanizes us. It is unavoidable and potentially salvific. My mother, Dot, always said we grow in wisdom and virtue through suffering and sacrifice.

There are many recurring elements in the Liturgical seasons, which overlap one another, and that is the way this book is constructed. We find some of these in the form of spiritual obstacles, such as pettiness, busyness, noise, and superficiality. On the other side, we find joy, childlike wonder, leisure, and holiness.

The intensity of these universal themes are highlighted as parts of the Liturgical seasons, but are not restricted to a particular time of year. The Blessed Trinity is not restricted by time and place as we are. You cannot say, "I have to wait until Lent to convert." Conversion can happen at any moment! You need to go to the Blessed Sacrament and, in silence, allow the Holy Spirit to shape those ordinary experiences so they make sense for you.

This book is not meant to be read from cover to cover. I recommend keeping it at your bedside and referencing it when you want to grow in *spiritual maturity* within any of the spiritual traits identified throughout. Refer to it often, because the value is in repetition. As the great French writer Francois Mauriac—one of the great, twentieth-century minds of Roman Catholicism—put it, "If you would tell me the heart of a man, tell me not what he reads, but what he rereads."

The Baltimore Catechism was about receiving the correct answers, but that's not the goal of genuine spirituality. My spiritual mentor, Daniel Murray, taught me spiritual direction was not in the answers but in the questions, which is best affirmed by the Rainer Maria Rilke quote, "...have patience with everything that is unsolved in your heart and to try to **cherish the questions themselves**..."[6]

Spiritual maturity is the ability to live with the questions. Sometimes those questions linger for five years, because you have not received a self-satisfying answer. You still have to pick up the pieces and live your life. Eventually though, faith, memory, and love are what rise to heal the suffering of loss.

A spiritually mature person remains steadfast in the darkness, knowing he or she may never receive the answers for which he or she yearns until he or she gets to the other side.

I ask that you begin your growth in spiritual maturity by asking yourself the below questions. Any time you feel the urge to focus on your spiritual maturity but do not know where to begin, turn to them. They will guide you. Godspeed in your journey to be holy and to be loved.

1. Who am I?
2. Where have I come from?
3. Where am I going?
4. What is prayer?
5. Who are the Father, Son, and Holy Spirit for me?
6. Where do I belong?
7. How can I be of service?
8. How can I become aware of divine presence in my life?
9. How can I have some assurance that my decisions about work, money, and relationships are made in a spiritually mature way according to my present circumstances?

10. How do I know that my life is lived in obedience to Jesus, the Master Teacher, and not just in response to my own impulses and desires?
11. Should I live a simpler life?
12. How do I listen attentively to the impulse of the Holy Spirit? What am I hearing right now?
13. How do I find joy? How do I find truth?
14. What gifts do I have to share?
15. What do I do when loneliness takes up residence in my life?
16. Why am I so needy for affection and approval?
17. How do I overcome my fears, my addictions, and my sense of failure or inadequacy?
18. Where is grace active in my life right now?
19. What question persists in my daily life?
20. When in my life has a painful or persistent question been dismissed or answered glibly by others?
21. What questions do I ask of Jesus; of life itself?
22. What teachings do I share with those who do not know Jesus?
23. Is the image of Jesus as a lamb meaningful to me?

Spiritual guidance affirms the basic quest for meaning. It calls for the creation of inner space in which the validity of the questions does not depend on the availability of answers but on the questions' capacity to open us to new perspectives and horizons. We must allow all the daily experiences of life—joy, laughter, tears, loneliness, fear, anxiety, insecurity, doubt, ignorance, the need for intimacy and affection, support, understanding, and the long cry for love—to be recognized as an essential part of the spiritual quest.

❧ I ❧
THE ADVENT SEASON

Secular society begins the new year on Jan. 1, but the sacred society of the church begins the new year on the first Sunday of Advent—typically at the end of November.

How I yearn for the whole world to celebrate a do-nothing Advent and then have a nothing-but-Christ Christmas.

Advent is an empty season—the quiet, still season when we refuse to be preoccupied with anything but the coming of Jesus. It is important to keep Advent as still and uncluttered as possible so we will be awake and ready when Jesus comes. Advent cautions us against flirting with the fierce and fiery mystery of Jesus's becoming man, of Jesus dwelling in our midst.

The spiritual life begins by waking up to the love and guidance of the Holy Spirit. Stay awake, be alert, be attentive, be on guard, be vigilant to the many times and many ways God comes to visit.

Let us pray that our eyes will be watchful and our hearts expectant during the holy season of preparation for the coming of our Lord and savior, Jesus, who will dispel the cold and darkness with His light and warmth.

For nine months, Jesus grew in his Mother's body. By His own will, she formed Him from herself, from the simplicity of her daily life. She had nothing to give Him but herself. This time of Advent is absolutely essential to our full attention, too. If we have truly given our humanity to be changed into Jesus, it is essential to us that we do not disturb this time of growth.

St. Paul, in his first letter to the Thessalonians, instructs us to "Rejoice always!" That's clear enough, isn't it? It doesn't say, "Rejoice sometimes!" It doesn't say, "Rejoice when times are good and the economy is strong!" It doesn't even say, "Rejoice during the Advent and Christmas seasons!" It simply says, "Rejoice always!"

The third Sunday of Advent is known as Gaudete Sunday. We light a pink candle on the Advent wreath as a reminder that, in the midst of the otherwise reflective season of Advent, the coming of the Lord, which we are preparing to celebrate, is a season of great joy, of nonstop prayers, and of constant thanks.

Advent invites us to rejoice in the Holy Spirit, who will rest upon us and renew us, especially those parts of ourselves that seem dead and betrayed, or even cut off.

"When there is a tendency to compartmentalize the spiritual and make it resident in a certain type of life only, the spiritual is apt gradually to be lost."
–Flannery O'Connor[7]

As adults, we can lose the spiritual fruit of joy—granted to us by the Holy Spirit—so easily:

- fighting crowds in traffic
- not enough sleep
- not getting everything done on our daily checklists
- spending too much money
- eating and drinking too much

This is no way to prepare the way of the Lord, to make His path to us free of all obstacles.

One of these obstacles is the impatient child still alive in all of us. Advent is a time of waiting. Yet we live in an infantile culture and we have immense trouble with waiting.

The advance of technology has made everything instantly available. We want everything to be immediate—meals, wealth, wisdom, spiritual fulfillment. In today's world, if we have to wait, we bring on stress in our lives. The question has to be asked, "What drives our lives? Is it technology or the natural order?"

John the Baptist announced the presence of Christ to a waiting world and he had the grace to see that presence in Jesus of Nazareth. We have to slow down, take the time to pray so we can, in the midst of this busy season, recognize Christ in our own lives. If we can do that, we would have no problem rejoicing and giving thanks.

The prophet Isaiah has a vision of our world turned upside down—a world of reversals when captives will be freed, when the hungry will be fed, when the selfish rich will be cut down to size. However, this is a vision of a future world. How do we react in the meantime as we are still anticipating this reversal? Right now, everything seems to be in turmoil.

No matter how much darkness, a light has come into our world. Jesus Christ delivers us from hopelessness. The world cannot extinguish this light and that is the reason for our being joyful, as Jesus said to his disciples, "I have told you this so that my joy may be in you and your joy may be complete." (John 15:11).

In his work, *Starlight: Beholding the Christmas Miracle All Year Long*, John Shea draws wonderful parallel of the Advent season readying the believer for the miracle of Christmas by telling us to "Behold!"

- "And behold, you shall be silent and unable to speak..." (Luke 1:20)[8]
- "Behold, you will conceive..." (Luke 1:31)
- "...behold, magi from the east arrived in Jerusalem..." (Matthew 2:1)
- "...behold, the angel of the Lord appeared to Joseph in a dream..." (Matthew 2:13)
- "And behold, the star that they had seen at its rising preceded them..." (Matthew 2:9)
- "Behold, the virgin shall be with child..." (Matthew 1:23)
- "...behold, I proclaim to you good news of great joy that will be for all the people." (Luke 2:10)

In the celebration of the Eucharist right before Holy Communion is distributed, the priest elevates the consecrated host and proclaims to the congregation robustly, "Behold, behold the lamb of God who takes away the sins of the world, blessed are those who are called to the supper of the Lamb."

To behold means to take a long, loving look at the real presence of Jesus in the Eucharistic host. It is the highest form of prayer and worship.

This contemplative gesture enables us to receive the Eucharist, despite being fully aware of our own unworthiness; also, fully aware that Jesus, the bread of life, is the greatest gift in the world.

1
JOY

To sum up the Advent season in a quick phrase, it is the anticipation of something joyful to come. Joy is a characteristic virtue of the season.

We are joyful during Advent because we experience the best of the past, present, and future, all gathered together in an explosive moment of ecstasy. A calm, faithful expectancy reigns in the scriptures proclaimed, in this holy season of childlike wonder, and of hope in each of our hearts.

Joy is lacking and fleeting in most people's lives, today. Yet, it is also one of the twelve fruits of the Holy Spirit and the first of the twelve most common dispositions of the spiritually mature life. The ability to be connected and sustain joy is a great challenge in a hectic, noisy, busy, crowded world. Preoccupation and distraction are constant forces of interference to establishing joy. One simply cannot say, "Come Hell or high water, I'm going to be happy, today."

Jesus never taught anyone how to pray. He was even reluctant to teach us how to pray the Lord's Prayer. Why is that? Well, it's because if we make a decision to live life abundantly, we will pray and as a result, we will discover joy. That is why joy is a fruit, a disposition, and a consequence—not a goal to be reached.

It's hard to differentiate for a lot of people, because it is human nature to be goal oriented. The cliché counter to being goal oriented is discovering how to be comfortable in our own skin—for instance, letting go of perfectionism and control.

One of the most common confessions of Catholics today is the sin of being judgmental. What's the medicine to take to be less judgmental? Being at peace with ourselves allows us to become more tolerant of the flaws of other people, and less judgmental as a result.

In the spiritual life, despite tragedy, hardship, and setback, one can still experience joy. A great example comes from Joshua David Stone's *Soul Psychology: Keys to Ascension*, where he theorizes, "Nothing outside of yourself causes you to think of feel anything. It is your interpretation, your belief, your perception of the situation that cause you to feel the way you do. For example, in the 1929 stock market crash, one person might have jumped out of the window of a building to commit suicide. Another person who lost a million dollars might have said, 'Easy come, easy go.'"[9]

Money came easy to that man and it was no sweat when he lost possibly more than anybody else. That is an example of pure, unadulterated joy in someone's life. He can maintain his composure, no matter the circumstances.

I've had experiences with people who understand deep grief. Those people were deeply in love and deeply attached to someone or something and they became inconsolably paralyzed by grief for the better part of twenty years. They simply stopped living life. That's a crystal-clear example of the absence of joy.

Jesus cautions us strongly not to let our hearts be shaped in the following fashion and wallow in spiritual immaturity:

> ***Hard-heartedness*** *– Jesus rails against people who are hard-hearted; that is, those who are not receptive to the ways and will of God*
> ***Half-heartedness*** *– Jesus has an allergic reaction to those who live mediocre, lukewarm lifestyles*
> ***Cold-heartedness*** *– people who ice their hearts and show no compassion or concern for other people*
> ***Heavy-heartedness*** *– Jesus does not want us to walk around with a millstone weighing down our hearts. He desires to unburden us from worry, fear, anxiety, bitterness, resentment, unforgiveness. His yoke is easy and His burden is light if we are willing to be yoked with Jesus*

Jesus desires to shape our hearts in this fashion, in a progressive manner, to enable us to sustain spiritual maturity:

> ***Light-heartedness*** *– Jesus is the light of the world. He dispels all darkness and enables us to live holy hilarity*
> ***Broken-heartedness*** *– Jesus challenges us to open ourselves up in crucified vulnerability, but not become a milquetoast and let people take advantage of us*
> ***Purity of heart*** *– "Blessed are the pure in heart, for they will see God." (Matthew 5:8)*[10]

Jesus wants us to remain lighthearted, to risk being brokenhearted, and to strive for purity of heart. Purity of heart involves childlike wonder, generosity, boundless forgiveness, and love for the less fortunate. Save the blessed mother and a few saints, no one fully achieves purity of heart—that is why I use the word "strive."

Those two steppingstones—lightheartedness and broken

heartedness—are integral. However, the people who hate those types of loose ends show up in droves, namely control freaks and perfectionists.

To say achieving purity of heart is so difficult does not make it hopeless. This is a marathon. When we establish lightheartedness early on in our spiritual journeys, we get into the habit of not taking ourselves too seriously. Broken heartedness is an adult willingness to be vulnerable to life's ups and downs—in good times and in bad. The prime example is two imperfect people who love each other. They get angry at each other, they get petulant, and they get hurt. The irony is, the person we love the most is the one who can hurt us the most.

When something is most personal, it has the potential to also have a universal application. Therefore, it is only when we make ourselves carefree enough to be light and vulnerable enough to be broken that we can ultimately be free.

Even if things seem awful, we can and should seek out humor. Everybody likes being around a person who is lighthearted—the one who can make an appropriate, funny remark that diffuses all stress and tension.

The bible is full of towering Advent figures. The prophet Isaiah is the first Advent figure. Then you have John the Baptist, the Blessed Mother, and finally, Jesus. These individuals are an inspiration to find joy in the perennial presence of the Lord.

"You will show me the path to life, abounding joy in your presence, the delights at your right hand forever." (Psalm 16:11)

2
SILENCE

God's first language is silence and everything else is a poor translation. Jewish theologian Abraham Joshua Heschel said, "God is of no importance unless He is of supreme importance." Silence is the pregnant backdrop against which all meaning shines forth.

If we do not have a wellspring of silence within us, we cannot understand our world, philosophy, theology, poetry, literature, music, mysticism ... we cannot understand ourselves, others, or God Himself.

Sweet silence, speak your word to me. Only a person who has something to say can keep silent. Out of long-guarded speechlessness comes the utterance of the thinker.

Three significant demons that we all have to wrestle are noise, busyness, and crowds.

The tragic loss of courtesy, politeness, and civility is growingly evident in our society. Notice the t-shirts, the bumper stickers, and the entertainment industry—not to mention social media! The prevailing attitude seems to be the more vulgar, the ruder, the more offensive, the more shocking ... the better.

We are a society of men and women sated with words and

starved for silence. The stronger my faith, the deeper God's word is able to penetrate my being. Contemplation deepens personality, strengthens convictions, results in serene detachment ... it aids interior liberty and promotes spiritual growth and emotional maturity.

Both in silent contemplation and in daily life, moreover, the contemplative must imitate Christ's radical and complete self-emptying.

One cannot attain anything in the spiritual life without total dedication, continued effort, experienced guidance, and real discipline.

When a person breaks away from his or her spiritual moorings, he or she becomes more and more superficial. Rootlessness leads to ruthlessness, and yet, with the Holy Spirit, we are but dust and chafe.

The first concern of a true follower of Christ must not be to enlarge his or her field of activity, but to deepen his or her interior life, subsuming everything within the great-souled, absorbing pursuit of a transforming union with God.

The seeds of sanctity and contemplation have been sown by God in each of our souls, but they remain dormant within many. This is where silence and inner reflection come into play. Sure, youth and pride are enticing, but wisdom is fulfilling to the highest degree. Perhaps it is captured best in Lin Yutang's metaphoric approach to the seasons...

> *"I like spring, but it is too young. I like summer, but it is too proud. So, I like best of all autumn, because its leaves are a little yellow, its tone mellower, its colors richer, and it is tinged a little with sorrow. Its golden richness speaks not of the innocence of spring, nor of the power of summer, but of the mellowness and kindly wisdom of approaching age. It knows the limitations of life and is content."*[11]

3

ANTICIPATION

Advent is the season of anticipation—in other words, the season of waiting. We are challenged to be calm, silent, hopeful, and trusting. So, the questions we must ask ourselves are, how do I wait? Do I wait with silence or am I waiting in angst, worry, and distraction? Can I wait with calmness? Can I wait with hopefulness? Can I wait not knowing how this is all going to turn out? We are invited to maintain a calm peacefulness, where it's not going to be perfect, but we'll have the flexibility to adjust for whatever it is to come.

The Universal Prayer of the Church instructs us to be silent and still in the morning and before drifting off to sleep. It is recommended to set aside at least one other time in the middle of the day to repeat that habit consciously.

Some people have prayer corners in their houses. They know that they have to go to that place. They have a rhythm of going to that place at a particular time and that enables them to engage the chaos—planned or unplanned—in the day.

Per the Liturgy of the Hours—the universal prayer of the

church—morning prayer begins, "God, come to my assistance. Make haste to help me."

When a spiritually mature person wakes up in the morning, he or she recognizes the uncertainty of how the day will unfold; however, he or she believes in divine assistance; therefore, no matter what the day throws at him or her, he or she will be unfazed.

If we have a deep, growing relationship with Father, Son, and Holy Spirit, we'll be able to recognize any unexpected event as a moment of grace rather than a moment of irritating frustration or an unwelcome intrusion.

At the end of the day, the last hour of the Liturgy of the Hours is also known as night prayer, which uses a different verse, and I believe it should be wired into everybody's brains. We pray,

"Into your hands, oh Lord, I commend my spirit." That's derived from Psalm 31:5. It means, "All the good that happened in the course of this day, as well as all the setbacks and hardships I've encountered ... I'm handing them all over to the Lord."

Why? Because I *anticipate* a good night's sleep. That's the alpha and the omega to the spiritually mature person's life: to wake up and go to bed with confidence in divine assistance. The universal church invites us to allow that beginning and end to set the rhythm for the middle of the day.

All good habits must be repeated. We can all get into a rut, but if we can keep it simple, keep it creative, keep it playful, then we're not going to get into obsessive-compulsive patterns of thinking, acting, and behaving.

Connect the written word of God with real-life experience, *while* anticipating divine help. That gets us to the next day and able to start over again without being worn down by old baggage.

Uptightness dissipates when anticipation of divine assistance is good practice. From a spiritual standpoint, that practice consists of being attentive and receptive to grace. If God loves us, he's going to try to connect with us ten thousand times a day. If we recognize twenty times in which He made an attempt to get our attention, we're going to have a banner day! Some people don't even catch it once for a day, two days, or a week.

It's a cooperative enterprise. St. Ignatius and St. Augustine both said, "Pray as though everything depended on God; act as though everything depended on you."[12] And, of course, there's that old saying, "God helps those who help themselves." There's a strong grain of truth in that, but He does have the ability to help people who aren't.

In Graham Green's novel, *The Power and the Glory*, the main character is an alcoholic priest. The smell of alcohol in his breath emanates from the pages. His depression reaches into the reader's soul. He feels worthless and like an abysmal failure. One day, he gets a sick call from a dying woman. He doesn't think he has a thing to give to this woman. Somehow, he musters up the courage to go, still feeling worthless, helpless, and like he has nothing to give. He sits and listens to her and then goes through the ritual of anointing her. At the end of their time together, the dying woman could not thank this whiskey priest enough.

All he did was simply show up and God's grace came to his rescue. So, grace can overcome, but from most people's vantage point, it would be insurmountable obstacle. St. Thomas Aquinas lived by the medieval maxim that "grace perfects and builds on nature."[13] If our human nature is healthy and wholesome, grace will take advantage of that condition and make us really lively, active, healthy, wholesome people.

Ask yourself, do you thank God when things go well? Do you blame God when things don't go well?

In times of crisis especially, we must remember six steps: stay prayerful, stay safe, stay healthy, stay steadfast, stay hopeful, and stay playful. We must anticipate what is to come and if our anticipation is right, even in a short amount of time, we will make the right decisions.

The spiritually mature person wakes up and goes to bed in prayer, believing in divine assistance. Therefore, throughout her day, he or she is able to remain mindful of his or her safety, health, faith, and hope. Most importantly, he or she doesn't take him- or herself too seriously. He or she ponders the question each day: what is the spiritual condition of my heart?

4
STILLNESS

French philosopher Blaise Pascal famously said, "All of humanity's problems stem from man's inability to sit quietly in a room alone." The moment most people wake up, before they even put their feet on the floor, their minds are racing regarding all they have to do!

There is a relationship between silence, stillness, solitude, and solidarity. We need to be silent to quiet all the competing voices in our heads: wife, children, boss, neighbors, siblings. The goal should be to identify and listen to the voice of Father, Son, and Holy Spirit. That takes effort, especially in our frenetic, noisy world. The most serious pollution to the spiritual life is noise pollution. Silence is the only remedy. Learning to grow in silence is the springboard to growing in stillness.

As soon as the phone rings, we have been conditioned to want to answer it right away. Technology has made us anything but still. When we remove the noise and clutter, we can finally discover who we truly are. That's why Jesus spent a lot of time in out-of-the-way places.

We all need to step away to a lakeside or a mountain and

reconnect in silence and stillness. It is the interior rudder to stabilize and balance in the midst of turmoil.

Spiritual maturity demands finding a rhythm, a routine, and a ritual to incorporate silence, stillness, solitude, and solidarity.

This takes discernment and discipline. Discernment is knowing what is already on our plates for the day. If I know early in the morning my day will be busy, it should be clear that I need to devote *more time* to **sitting** in silence—perhaps ten or fifteen minutes, rather than the five I had previously planned.

Hopefully, there's some energy left at the end of the day to reflect on daily experiences. The church has always encouraged a quick examination of conscience. If we don't do this every day, our daily experiences will be on top of us instead of us being on top of them, which dehumanizes us.

It is said English romantic poet William Wordsworth walked several miles before breakfast.[14] Walking is a spiritual discipline, but we don't have to be world-class walkers like Wordsworth or John Adams. Walking clears the head, but we must remain attentive to it, just like everything else. Sometimes we have to drop what we're doing, especially when we're caught in a mental block, to take a ten-to-fifteen-minute walk. Give it a try. I trust you'll come back fresh and be more productive and fruitful.

Personally, the more time I spend in stillness, the more I notice all the things fall into place. That is time tested and a universal truth.

Yet, there is a dark side to stillness. Sister Macrina Wiederkehr wrote, "I have never felt very docile, yet I have my moments, and today is one of them, when I think I could hand over anything God would ask for. I know myself well enough not to say that too loudly, but the yearning is here. Perhaps this is the reason I run so much. A part of me is terrified of what I will hear in stillness."[15]

We're afraid of what we'll discover in silent contemplation. How will it change the way we're living? That is what keeps us from stillness, silence, solitude, and solidarity. We're not willing to pay the price of changing our patterns of living and thinking. We get ourselves into a mechanical pattern of living known as comfort.

Quiet contemplation transforms worry into wonder. It even transforms the idea of foes in our minds into friends in our neighborhoods. Have the awareness to adjust your perception of people and show up in the world loving more.

The 8 Dispositions of Advent

Awake

Still

Empty

Joyful

Hopeful

Secret Revealed

Full of Grace

Pregnant With Christ

❧ II ☙
THE CHRISTMAS SEASON

The story is an ancient one, but the glory remains ever new and undimmed. Jesus, our Lord and savior, is the light of the world.

The church prays, "Through the night hours of the darkened earth, we, Your people, Lord, watch for the coming of Your promised Son." Now, the watch is over. Isaiah proclaims it, "For a child is born to us, a son is given to us; upon his shoulder dominion rests. They name him Wonder-Counselor, God-Hero, Father-Forever, Prince of Peace." (Isaiah 9:5)

An angel of the Lord startled shepherds with the Good News, "For today in the city of David a savior has been born for you who is Messiah and Lord." (Luke 2:11).

The Good News proclaimed by the prophet Isaiah and the angel of the Lord is that Jesus did not run away from our darkness. He set up residence right in the middle of the darkness of uncertainty, of being lost, of being afraid, of being blind to His grace, of being in sin. Now, we who walked in darkness have seen a great light. No matter how deep our darkness, Jesus is deeper still when He took on flesh and all sin in the world.

Christmas is the mystery of Jesus taking on our flesh. Holiness, sleeping in the womb of the Virgin Mary, is now born to us—the Creator of Life being created! Because of this light, everything becomes clear to those who have faith. For those who do not believe, the darkness remains as a veil clouding their vision.

Christmas is a feast day for the child in all of us—a time to release the child within. It is a time for pondering the impact of one child on history, pondering the impact the Christ-child has on our lives.

Mirabile Visu: in the Christ-child, our Heavenly Father chose to need us. He chose to need every one of us. The profound vulnerability of the baby born in Bethlehem as He divests himself of glory in order to assume the form of fragility. This is the core message of Christmas.

Babies grow up, and so did Jesus. From youth to adulthood, we are told Jesus grew in wisdom, stature, and grace. He asserted his independence clearly by distancing Himself from his parents in the temple at twelve years old; by making a whip and driving out moneychangers; excoriating religious leaders of His day because of their hypocrisy, corruption, and incompetence.

Ecce homo: behold, Jesus the man! Does that mean His childhood was left behind? No. The Gospels give us good reason to believe that the first years of Jesus's life occupy a privileged place in our interpretation of the rest of his Good News.

How can Christ's childhood hold such simple and profound meaning? Jesus repeatedly acknowledges childhood as the defining mark of everyone's humanity: "Amen, I say to you, unless you turn and become like children, you will not enter the kingdom of heaven. Whoever humbles himself like this child is the greatest in the kingdom of heaven." (Matthew 18:3-4).

The Gospels clearly teach that Jesus came to make us beloved sons and daughters and that means we cannot understand the incarnation properly if we miss that Jesus the man never ceased to be Jesus the child.

Consider the neediness of a child. Throughout Jesus's entire adult ministry, we see that He retains childlike neediness. He depends on people to feed him; Zaccheus, Martha, and Mary, and the Pharisee; He has no place to lay His head. Jesus did not own a home, a townhouse, a condo, a lakeside bungalow; He depends on Joseph of Arimathea to give him a tomb.

Jesus remains the invisible child concealed in the sacraments and awaiting our response to His grace. It should not surprise us that when we encounter Christ today, we find Him chiefly in the needy and helpless of this world; the lost, the least, the lonely, the voiceless, the defenseless, the widow, the orphan, the rejected, the stranger.

Children are weak, helpless, needy; but they are not quiet. They demand love—care, affection, and attention that will satisfy their hearts.

Mirabile Visu: Jesus needs each one of us to extend a hand in service, in kindness, in generosity, in forgiveness, in healing, and in love in order to make the world a better place.

The Christmas revelation is clear: light conquers darkness, warmth defeats cold, fruitfulness replaces bareness. No matter how pervasive the darkness of the outer world—pandemic, war, famine, tsunami, floods, and other natural and manmade disasters—the radiant, glorious, transcendent light of the world, the baby born in Bethlehem, the crucified Christ, the Risen Lord prevails.

Of course, I desire everyone to have what Christmas cards and carols say: holy nights full of peace, unity, beauty, wonder, mystery, truth, goodness, joy, and love. But that is not what we always get. Christmas arrives each year to find our health weak and diminished, our careers or vocations under stress, our finances dipping badly, our relationships in need of repair, or our world more divided, hostile, and crazy.

A baby—any baby—born helps us to better distinguish between what matters most and what matters least. This is true even more so with the baby born in Bethlehem. That is one reason why we celebrate the birth of Jesus every year—so we can be restored and renewed again. The Christmas season challenges us to seek truth, crave goodness, allow ourselves to be moved by beauty, and begin to live life abundantly once again.

5

CHILDLIKE WONDER

There is a story about a little boy who, one evening after supper, asked his dad to read a book to him. The father was comfortably resting in his La-Z-Boy chair watching his favorite show and told his son to see him later. The little boy persisted. Finally, the father went into his desk and pulled out a map of the world. He cut the map into jigsaw pieces, scattered them over the glass-top coffee table, and told his son to put the map together, come back when he was done, and the father would read him the book.

The father felt relieved, thinking it would take his son at least two to three hours to put the map of the world together. In ten minutes, the boy returned, telling his father he was finished. The father was amazed when he saw the map of the world put together and asked his son how he did it so quickly.

The boy answered, "Dad, on the other side there was a picture of a family, so I put the family together and when the family was right, the world was right."

In most cases, it is within the family that we learned to walk and speak. We learned a measure of security, self-confidence, and independence. We came to a sense of ourselves and acquired an ability to appreciate others. We came to have faith in God and a sense of his presence.

"Because you are God's chosen ones, holy and beloved, clothe yourselves with heartfelt mercy, with kindness, humility, meekness, and patience." (Colossians 3:12).[16]

We need these virtues in our homes more than we need consumer goods. These virtues are spiritual clothing for us. Blessed is the family wrapped in the warmth of these virtues. It takes a lot of spiritual courage and spiritual strength to make any family work, last, and grow.

Joseph, Mary, and Jesus became a Holy Family for all of us because they did not seek their own individual, personal wills to be done, but because they lived for God and one another. They dedicated themselves to adjusting and readjusting, when necessary, to doing God's will as well as they could. God was always at the center of their lives.

Celebrating the Feast of the Holy Family is a good opportunity to reflect on family life today. Families are the pillars of our society. Family life has been under attack these days despite politicians proclaiming the need for family values. Television mocks, ridicules, and insults wholesomeness in family life—the increase of divorce, the unemployed father, the depressed mother, the pregnant daughter, and the drug-addicted son all contribute to breakdown as well as financial, emotional, and moral stress and strain on the family.

Childlike wonder is a disposition you can draw out of yourself that tempers your thought patterns. A child discovers tickling her parents and never tires of that little activity. Eventually, she'll come upon an occasion where she is told, "Not now," and all of a sudden, she's shocked into "What do you mean, 'Not now?'" We should plunge into play because it is always available. She's hurt because she's disoriented. Her orientation is, as soon as she wakes up, play is the priority of the day. There's nothing else to distract her or preoccupy her. There are no obstacles.

As adults, we should create days as children do, not allowing time and space to constrict us. What a radically different way of living a day! That's what retirement is supposed to look like, but rest assured, we are meant to have that type of abundance in the here and now.

That's why I admired my grandfather. He was playful each and every day. That was his guiding rule. He didn't allow duty, responsibility, work, or money to disrupt him.

People can become obsessive compulsive about not having enough money. Credit cards can easily exploit people. They are the landmines disrupting our adventure. Despite that, an examination of conscience at the end of the day—that's a spiritual practice—could be as simple as asking yourself, "How many times did I laugh today?"

A 4-year-old girl was in the presence of her mother and father, who just brought home her baby brother. After she had the opportunity to meet the newest member of the family and the baby was put down for the night, this little girl asked her parents if she could speak to her baby brother in private. The parents, a little puzzled, granted her wish and left the room, listening quietly at the cracked door. The little girl approached the crib, leaned her head in as close as she could to her brother, and said, "I have a question. Can you tell me about God? Because, I'm starting to forget."

We are all born with wonder and it is a serious responsibility to find a way to sustain it. The major obstacle is when worry starts to creep into our minds. One of the best prayers I pray is, "Lord, fill me with wonder and free me from worry."

Children evoke wonder in us all. That's why grandparents are just head over heels when they can babysit their grandchildren.

If kids have that type of impact on us, why do we not seek out the child within us?

During the Christmas season, especially, a child's eyes are wide open, because he wants to see what everyone is excited about, what everyone is celebrating; yet, it is invisible to the naked eye. He has the chance to learn what the Creed proclaims: "I believe in things visible and invisible." That's what Christmas can reignite in every human being, even one living to one-hundred-and-two years old.

On Christmas Eve, that most special, grace-filled, Holy Night, we get a glimpse, see what is invisible, and believe in it. Every Christmas Eve, that same dynamic unfolds. It's a profound dynamic of discovery—the discovery of birth, the discovery of life, the discovery of love, the discovery of sadness, the discovery of pain and suffering, and the discovery that even death doesn't destroy the excitement of this night; because new life is the beginning step to eternal life.

Nora's Innocence

Five years old she is,
An older sister to her brother Danny.
A first born to her mom and dad.

Whenever she sees me on Sunday morning,
in chuch,
she smiles.

Her face lights up,
like a morning glory.

She knows my flaws.
I said, "animal cookies."
She corrected me with, "animal crackers."

She smiles again,
I think I am beginning to learn about grace.

6

INNOCENCE

In spring 1985, I was a resident priest at St. James in Elkins Park while teaching high school at Archbishop Kennedy in Conshohocken. Before going to school each morning, I celebrated the 6:30 a.m. mass. That April, brothers Kevin and Brian were assigned to serve mass for the first time.

They arrived on Monday morning at 6 a.m., bright-eyed and eager to perform all the tasks of serving at the altar. I assigned Brian to light the candles and Kevin to put out the cruets. They were not happy with this distribution of labor, each wanting to do everything and anything else.

On Tuesday morning, they arrived in the sacristy at 6:10 and were more than happy to share the duties of setting up.

Wednesday morning followed and they arrived at 6:20. Kevin instructed Brian to light the candles that day.

On Thursday, they arrived at 6:27. I had already lit the candles and set up.

Finally, on Friday morning, Kevin came in to the sacristy right before I was to go on the altar. I waited for him to get vested and asked of his brother's whereabouts. Kevin told me that Brian was too tired and decided to stay in bed. I asked

Kevin why he didn't do the same. With a look of innocence and sincerity, Kevin responded, "Father, then who is going to wash away your iniquities?"

Innocence is a necessary starting point, in the journey to spiritual maturity. It cannot be bypassed. We need to look back in our lives and be thankful for the times in which we enjoyed spontaneous innocence, because that will be the stepping stone to preventing us taking ourselves too seriously and getting tied up in self-absorption. The more that we can be free of egotism, the more we create space to give thanks, worship, and honor the Father, Son, and Holy Spirit. Our world is expanded.

Worship is essential for healthy living. It's tough to enter into worship when we don't have a memory of innocence. Innocence will not get us to the end, but it does get us out of the gate. We wouldn't believe if we didn't have innocence. Faith is enriched in the soil of innocence. The seed of innocence grows and helps nourish the soil of faith.

Naturally, innocence is most prevalent in childhood. Children don't have a scintilla of doubt about being loved and that's what gives them the freedom to explore. There's growing self-awareness without self-consciousness.

When the child does something spontaneous, such as placing his hand on a hot stovetop, his parents may react with either a rough grab or a slap on the hand. All of a sudden, that child is introduced to a world of judgment and rejection. That inability to process rejection can hold a person immature for 25 years! Now, he's either deathly afraid of being rejected or can never accept being rejected. His interpretation of criticism is a catastrophic rejection of not only what he did or said, but of his whole person.

Yet, there is a wolf in sheep's clothing: naivety. There is a significant, clear-cut difference between the two. The innocent response is the right response when there isn't an expectation of having requisite knowledge. Naivety is where we should be held accountable for knowing what's happening.

The great example is, "The dog ate my homework." Naivety resorts to this posture by not dealing honestly. Innocence is always spontaneous. Naivety is calculated. As soon as the naïve person gets called on the carpet, she automatically knows what she was doing. Naivety is when we try to convince ourselves we're innocent when we're not. We had the opportunity to know, but we chose to look the other way or chose not to be exposed out of fear.

Naivety has a range of detriment to it, where innocence is much like simplicity. Naivety is duplicity.

Without spiritual growth, innocence is suppressed, and the longer it is locked away in the depths of the soul, the more difficult it is to remember.

> "We shall not cease from exploration,
> and the end of all our exploring
> will be to arrive where we started
> and know the place for the first time."
> –T.S. Eliot, Little Gidding, The Four
>   Quartets[17]

Innocence is the sum of simple, little, playful encounters enabling a child to wake up and see everything as new and exciting.

Kids have to feel, taste, and experience everything. Give a child a $10 bill and watch as her eyes widen as if you gave her a million bucks! She can't contain her excitement. She might not even know it's a $10 bill. There's no value put on anything. It's just a gift and that's innocence.

Oscar Wilde said, "A cynic is a man who knows the price of everything and the value of nothing." As our lives go on, we can get jaded and cynical, which is the opposite of innocence. Children are free from putting monetary value on something—a cookie, candy, chocolate, a $10 bill ... All of those are gifts. A gift is received with surprise and excitement, wonder and awe.

Children simply have an abundance of excitement, delight, and enjoyment. They get so wound up that they don't just walk, they don't just run ... they bounce off the walls!

In the New Testament, there are two Greek words used for the idea of time. Chronos (χρόνος) is measured, linear time. Kairos (καιρός) is time outside of time, such as dream, wonder, and exploration—in other words, time spent.[18]

How much of your day was comprised of each type of time? When you're caught in your day looking at your watch a hundred times, you know you're not in a good space. Innocence is freed of the preoccupation with measured time and is filled up with time outside of time.

The travels of the shepherds in the field and the messages from the archangels are recounted in the infancy narratives of Matthew and Luke. Through these Gospels, we experience the miracle of birth, the mystery of life, the goodness of love in a human and divine exchange, and it is all occurring in this little stable, as there was no room for them in an inn. Now, though, there is cosmic room for them.

His birth brings about a cosmic change, a universal change, for all who come and see, all who begin to give thanks and praise, for all who worship this baby and allow this baby to keep them connected to joy, silence, anticipation, and stillness. The shepherds in the field represent the very poor and lowly, but they are now key players in this event. No one is excluded in this world of inclusivity, but it's not a patronizing inclusion. It's genuine.

7

SIMPLICITY

"Rewriting is very painful. You know it's finished when you can't do anything more to it, though it's never exactly the way you want it ... the hardest thing in the world is simplicity. And the most fearful thing, too. You have to strip yourself of all your disguises, some of which you didn't know you had. You want to write a sentence as clean as a bone. That is the goal."
–James Baldwin[19]

We are incapable of discovering simplicity on our own. The Holy Spirit will lead us to this spiritual treasure.

Simplicity is active trust in the Holy Spirit. We need to make a conscious decision to sell off sophistication and complexity and embrace simplicity. This will involve going against the current of our culture.

In 1995, Dr. Bob Moorehead, former pastor of Seattle's Overlake Christian Church, did just that when he wrote his essay, "The Paradox of Our Age" In it, Moorehead takes a deep dive into modern life.

"We spend more, but have less. We buy more, but enjoy

less. We have bigger houses and smaller families, more conveniences, but less time."[20]

These statements capture a perplexing paradox in the spiritual life. We can have few possessions and still be wealthy. When we depend solely on our own resources, we can easily get sidetracked and confuse what matters most and what matters least in life.

Moorehead continues, "We've learned how to make a living, but not a life. We've added years to life not life to years."[21]

The great danger of accumulating possessions is they possess us rather than us being in possession of them. A guy who drives his dream car but spends more time with it than his wife and children has become a slave to his possession.

"These are the days of two incomes, but more divorce; fancier houses, but broken homes," Moorehead states.[22]

There is something radically different when a first child is born and gives new meaning to a family. In this day and age, many families need both the man and woman to work. The debate for gender equality in the workplace and income equality must continue; however, it creates a paradox in the household. Fleeting thoughts of feeling unfulfilled, because we gave up on a degree to take care of the children fulltime, societal pressures to not be a stay-at-home mother or father, and financial stresses of only one working parent—these are all legitimate reasons, but there's a significant price to be paid as a result.

Moorehead concludes, "Give time to love, give time to speak and give time to share the precious thoughts in your mind."[23]

Busyness is one of the great diseases of our time. It is an immense spiritual poison. There's not enough time to get everything done in a twenty-four-hour period. Then we get stressed out because we didn't check off every item of our to-do lists for the given day.

Clutter overwhelms the brain. Even television is a contributor. We think we're taking a moment to unwind, but now we're more attached to the movie or the show than we are to the people watching it with us. A couple may go to a movie, but after the date, they should go out, get something to eat, and discuss it. No one should be too busy for that.

According to a 2019 survey, twenty-three percent of Americans attend church every week.[34] That means seventy-seven percent cannot even find one hour in their crowded lives on a consistent weekly basis. Kids don't go to mass because they have soccer, cheerleading, or travel team practice, and then they go to grandma's for dinner. We don't have ten minutes let alone one hour to carve out on Sunday for prayer with the community! We pay a spiritual price for that.

In talking to my community during the COVID-19 pandemic, I noticed two very specific things that spiked, which had not been common practices of late: sharing a meal with the whole family and playing board games after the meal! Those two pastimes present the opportunity to have fruitful conversation. Quarantine gave us time back that wasn't available and it was promising to see people using it to be playful and enjoy each other's company.

Self-awareness is key. If we are spiritually mature and welcome simplicity into our daily living, we have the incredible gift of not being oppressed by time. We are open and have the patience to truly listen to others. We can be free of political correctness. We can be spontaneous. We don't allow unfinished business to hold its grips on us like a ball and chain.

You know that simplicity is alive and well in you when you value the people that gather around the Christmas tree more than the gifts that are under it.

ashes ... dust...
a reminder of humus (earth)
a reminder of humanness
a call to be more human

we need that tap on the shoulder
that mark on the forehead
from time to time
that says:
"Hey, don't forget!
"You're redeemed!
"You are the image of the
Living God!"

with a smudge here and there
the telltale signs of a
passionate earthiness
from those times when you
let yourself live
and got your hands dirty
this indeed is the image of
the Living God

this is redemption
you are redeemed
you are deemed once again
holy, beautiful,
from God's own hand
it is a time to celebrate
the mystery of death and
rising from the ash...
of living the image of God
the ultimate mystery
of a God embracing humanness
and a human embracing God.

❧ III ❧
THE LENTEN SEASON

The season of Lent is a season of repentance, renewal, and fulfillment. The forty days of Lent should be a time when we hear God's call more clearly. Lent is a time to deepen our love and commitment to Father, Son, and Holy Spirit.

Prayer, fasting, and almsgiving are the traditional ways the church invites us to deepen our love. Almsgiving is recognized as the way to reorder relations with those in need. Prayer reorders our relationship with God and neighbor, especially the prayer of forgiveness. Finally, fasting helps us to experience the plight of so many people oppressed by hunger.

The mission of the church is a mission of reconciliation. The work of the church is the work of healing all the alienations: labor/management, East/West, conservatives/liberals, men/women, parents/teenagers, rich/poor. The list of divisions is almost limitless. The list of those committed to healing is painfully short, yet marked with ashes.

Lent begins with a challenge and an invitation to reform our lives and to believe in the Good News—turn from sin and be faithful to the Gospel. Marked with the ashes of our mortality and of human frailty, but with the sign of salvation as well, we enter this sacred space and time to confront anew the reality of ourselves and of our God. The intensity of this endeavor, like the scorching midday sun of the desert, has reduced our pretensions to fine ash, revealing the truer, deeper self.

There are other ashes we carry. They are the product of our human history and not necessarily of God's activity and grace. These are the ashes of low self-esteem and the resultant unfulfilled potential of our lives and ministry. These are the ashes of long-ago hurts and disappointments—real or imagined—yet very much unresolved. These are the ashes of sinful attitudes and patterns of behavior that we have accepted. These are the ashes of frustrated dreams of idealism and creativity forfeited in the wake of disillusionment.

They disfigure our real human dignity, obscure the divine life within each of us, bury us beneath their accumulated weight until we encounter the Living One whose baptismal bath cleanses us and raises us from the death of our former selves to newness of life.

Lent is the church's annual, forty-day retreat. It is a time to strip away the superficiality, pettiness, busyness, and noise and discover once again what is really important—divine love and human love. Lent is a time to check our priorities and determine who or what is primary in our lives. It is a time to worship God more fervently and give Him our first fruits and not just the leftovers of our talent, energy, and time.

During the Lenten season, we must ask ourselves, "What is one thing I should change, but keep putting off?"

Many of us desire to grow in holiness, grow closer to our Lord, become more like Him through prayer, fasting, and acts of charity. However, by the fifth week of Lent, our enthusiasm wanes. We just hope we make it to Holy Week. As Jesus was tested for forty days in the desert, we too are challenged to remain faithful for the full duration of the Lenten season. The final days can be the most difficult. They can also be the most grace-filled. How? When we exhaust our own resources, we are more likely to turn to the Lord for help. We beg for assistance. The plea from the psalmist, **"make haste to help me"** takes on a whole new meaning.

Lent is a time for waking up—a time to shake off the fog from our minds, to get the sand out of our eyes, so that we can sit up and see clearly the spiritual condition of our souls.

> *Memento, homo, quia pulvis es, et in pulverem reverteris* –
> Remember, man, what dust you are and to dust you will return (Genesis 3:17-19).

How to Fast and Feast in Modern Times

FAST from	**FEAST on**
Complaining	Gratitude
Worry	Wonder
Bitterness	Forgiveness
Gloom	Beauty
Discouragement	Hope
Gossip	Silence
Fear	Faith
Social Media	Sacred Scripture
Pettiness	Patient Tolerance
Sin	Virtue

8
SUFFERING LOVE

Suffering love is a lived experience. It is felt throughout the five senses to the very core of the soul. To be able to live in our pain and still have the disposition of faith, mercy, and love, is a true testament to spiritual maturity.

We all experience this feeling at various points throughout our lives. It yanks the hairs on top of our heads, tugs on our heartstrings, rips through the very fabric of our souls; however, once we are finished dying to ourselves, we rise to become more elevated versions of ourselves. We need to make our suffering love like Jesus's suffering, death, burial, and rising, in order to gain a spiritually mature perspective on all that is around us. It is true what St. Paul said in his epistle to the Philippians. Our attitudes must be Christ's.

At baptism, we begin a lifetime of growing into redemptive death with Jesus. We keep hidden our pain, our suffering, the injustices, the loneliness, the bitter disappointments in other people, ourselves, and the church. We rely on Jesus to be with us as we walk with Him on our own road to Calvary.

In one of his most recognized works, *A Farewell to Arms*, Ernest Hemingway wrote, "The world breaks everyone, and afterwards many are strong at the broken places."[24] And in his analysis of Hemingway's work, Rabbi Sidney Greenberg reflected, "Whether or not we become strong in the broken places depends ultimately on our attitude toward trouble. If we realize that suffering is our common human lot and that it can help us grow in spirit and in understanding, then we can indeed use it to grow strong in the broken places."[25]

One of the most common experiences of human suffering is death. The church, in her wisdom, invites us to meditate on the meaning and mystery of death every time we celebrate the Eucharist. Anyone who attempts to live the paschal mystery—that is the birth, life, suffering, and death of Jesus—will acknowledge the mysterious call to die in order to live.

Suffering—our own or that of a loved one—is perhaps the greatest test of faith we will face, for it seems invariable to raise the basic question: "How can this be happening if there is a God who is both all-powerful and all-loving?" For if God is all-powerful and allows this pain, then God is not all-loving; or if the all-loving God wants to stop this suffering but cannot, then God is not all-powerful.

A spiritually mature person replaces inconsolable mourning with comfort in times of tragedy and loss. In his *Letters and Papers from Prison*, Lutheran pastor, theologian, and anti-Nazi dissident Dietrich Bonhoeffer explains that while the absence of someone whom we love cannot be swept under the rug and ignored, patience and hope will help us triumph. Although it seems like an insurmountable task, we can and will make it through.

"It is nonsense to say that God fills the gap; God doesn't fill it, but on the contrary, keeps it empty and so helps us to keep alive our former communion with each other, even at the cost of pain."[26]

It is not always evident, but many times, faith requires discipline. I often recommend fasting as an additional way to strengthen and mature the spirit. Fasting is good for the soul as well as the body. It serves as a positive penance for spiritual enrichment.

There are three specific reasons why people in biblical times fasted. The first was repentance. They knew how deep sin sunk into their lives. The second reason people fasted was to remember or to mourn tragic events. For example, Daniel fasted when he remembered the destruction of Jerusalem. The third reason to fast is to rivet our attention on God. Are you ready to worship God right now? Do you have a sense of His presence?

When we fast, we say that there's more to us than just our appetites. Fasting challenges the addictions of the soul that society says are OK—namely shopping habits, eating habits, and sexual habits. Fasting helps us discover the contours of our souls and who we are before God.

Fasting is never an end itself; that's why it has so many different outcomes, but all the other outcomes are of no real value if compassion is not enlarged and extended through fasting.

To live a life of compassion is to follow Christ's example.

Minneapolis schoolteacher Donald Erlichmann was shot three times and murdered by three hitchhikers he and his son picked up one Sunday night in 1970. He was 47.

After the burial, Erlichmann's wife, Mary, wished to welcome the three unapprehended young men into her home. This was the kind of love, she believed, they could understand and need. To do so, she wrote "An Open Letter to the Three Boys Who Murdered My Husband."

> *"During the past three days my grief and desolation have been erased and comforted by the love and faith of so many wonderful friends and relatives, But, in the midst of this, and especially in the quiet moments, my thoughts keep turning to you three. You may feel that you are men, but to me you are just boys—like my own sons—and I*

> *wonder to whom you are turning for comfort and strength and reassurance.*
>
> *"I suppose I will never know what motivated your actions that night, but if the shots were fired out of sheer panic, my heart aches for you and I wish there were only some way I could help you in what you must be suffering now.*
>
> *"If hate made you pull that trigger, I can only pray that you can come to know the love of God that fills the heart and leaves no room for hate. If you were under the influence of drugs, please, for my sake and your own, don't waste your lives, too. Get help and rid yourselves of that stuff.*
>
> *"Please, if you see this, find a church some place where you can be alone; then read this again. Know that God forgives you and that my family and I forgive you—then go out and make something worthwhile out of the rest of your lives.*
>
> *"God keep and bless you."*[27]

Because of this great love, her own and God's, perhaps for even a brief moment, there was more peace and less war in that Minnesota city. My hope is that those three men discovered the Lord's love, stopped the wars inside themselves, and made something worthwhile out of the rest of their lives. That is the tremendous impact prayer, conversion, and grace can have on a suffering soul.

9

RECONCILIATION

Anyone remotely familiar with the Gospels senses immediately that there is something missing in our approach to conflict resolution. If Jesus were conducting a workshop on conflict resolution, where do you think He would start? On this matter He has made Himself perfectly clear. The foundation of peaceful human relationships is forgiveness. No wonder that in the only formal prayer that Jesus taught us—the Our Father—forgiving one another is at the very core, and every time Jesus urges us to forgive each other He connects our forgiving with asking God to forgive us.

There is, thus, a vertical and a horizontal dimension to forgiveness. The vertical dimension of God forgiving us rests on the horizontal dimension of our forgiving each other. What is really needed is not a succession of individual acts of forgiveness, as admirable as this is, but an interior state of forgiveness. We should try to maintain in ourselves a disposition of being ready to forgive each other. In this case, Jesus does in fact ask us to be divine.

Many people object to confession. "Why do I have to confess my sins to a priest? I can just go directly to God."

The priest represents the human being in us all. There's accountability to the sacrament of reconciliation and there's wisdom that we are acknowledging that we offended a certain number of people, but we don't' have the time and energy to go back and retrace our steps. Through this sacramental exchange, we enter the confessional weighed down by sin and we come out full of grace. That's the best tradeoff we can ever experience!

After confession, I tell people, "Right now, you are full of grace. So, you have two options: you can go outside and do three cartwheels to celebrate or go home and eat your favorite ice cream." We need to take time to celebrate the weight of the world being lifted off of our shoulders through the sacrament of reconciliation.

Medical research has shown that forgiveness can be good for a person's health while holding a grudge can be harmful.[28] The person who says, "I don't get angry, I get even," might, in fact, be punishing him- or herself as much as the intended victim. There is not only a religious impetus to forgive, but also therapeutic, social, and practical reasons to do so.

When Jesus looked up and saw Zacchaeus in the sycamore tree, He asked to stay with the tax collector from Jericho. Yet, as He frequently saw, Jesus was met with much skepticism from the bystanders.

"He has gone to stay at the house of a sinner." (Luke 19:7). Zacchaeus repented, telling Jesus he would give half his possessions to the poor and repay any extortions four times over.

"Today salvation has come to this house because this man too is a descendant of Abraham. For the Son of Man has come to seek and to save what was lost." (Luke 19:9-10).

How many are eager to meet Jesus in the sacrament of reconciliation? What is God's favorite daily miracle?

God's forgiving love endures from generation to generation. Jesus never tires telling us that He loves us, forgives us, and heals us.

We live today in a world so much in need of forgiveness. Sometimes we hurt so deeply that the pain retains its power for years. To love your enemies, to do good to those who hate you, and to pray for those who persecute you and make life miserable for you, are Jesus's great challenges.

Jesus tells the apostles, "If your brother sins, rebuke him; and if he repents, forgive him. And if he wrongs you seven times in one day and returns to you seven times saying, 'I am sorry,' you should forgive him."

To speak of sin by itself apart from grace is to forget the resolve of God. But to speak of grace without sin is surely no better. For the Catholic church and Catholic parents to ignore, euphemize, or otherwise mute the reality of sin is to cut the nerve of the Gospel. For the sober truth is that without full disclosure on sin, the Gospel of grace becomes unnecessary and uninteresting.

Forgiveness is the final measure of our love for one another. Though it is sometimes said that the forgiveness asked of us is beyond the human, the opposite is true: forgiveness is the most human act we can perform, for it springs from the truth of who we are: children created in the image and likeness of an all-loving and forgiving Father.

10
FALSE SELF VS. TRUE SELF

Faith gives us great light, but it does not remove all the darkness. That is why faith requires what I call "night vision."

Imagine yourself standing in a field. In your right hand is a golden thread at the end of which is a swan pulling you upward. In our left hand is a rusty chain. At the end of the rusty chain is a nasty dog pulling you in the opposite direction. Do you see yourself being pulled in conflicting ways?

Those without the desire or discipline to engage in the important work of self-knowledge or those unhappy with how they see themselves are inclined to let go of the rusty chain. This could be a mistake! We cannot grow by side-stepping the difficult. We are not the sole arbiter of what is good. Most importantly we are not either good or bad. We are both.

We may be inclined or advised to get rid of the nasty dog and fly off with the swan. Holding on to both thread and chain is the meaning of being an incarnate Christian. A biblical believer learns to hold these opposites in a healthy tension.

"Nasty dog" people can become entrapped in anger, cynicism, and bitterness. "Swan" people may fall into a delusion of being "holy," acting in ways that are merely superficial, never engaging in the messiness of real life. There is nothing attractive about that! Working toward spiritual maturity requires us to hold in creative tension the dark and light within us, to teach, if you will, the swan and the dog to befriend one another.

The dog has as much to contribute to our holiness as does the swan. It represents the dark side of our personalities and is dangerous only to the degree to which we refuse to acknowledge it, project it onto others, or ignore it altogether. It is the dark side of our lives that holds the treasure chest filled with the seeds of our unlived lives! It is precisely there that compassion, patience, and forgiveness are to be found.

It is only when we decide to let go and abandon the false self that conversion occurs. Now we are ready to be taught by Jesus. He teaches us His way—the way of vulnerable love. If we fail to die to the false self, we become a victim of what we deny.

It's a common misconception that we "reach" God by ridding ourselves of sin. Confession is to speak our full selves, our true selves that admit the weeds and the wheat of our souls. In humility, we bring our sinfulness to the Lord and His mercy touches us; we become touched sinners. So great is His love for us that Jesus takes that weakness and transforms it into strength. Gradually grace empowers us to name our demons without fear. This is the gift of discernment.

How do we proclaim truth to a world that operates largely by fraud and hypocrisy? This was the constant battle Jesus faced in His ministry. He knew full He would hand over His work to sinners, and it was the touched sinners—the saints—who carried on His message and made it a lived reality for generations to come.

> *"The saints are the bold ones, daring enough to be different, humble enough to make mistakes, wild enough to be burnt in the fire of divine love, real enough to make the rest of us see how enormously phony we are. They transform passion and raise it to a higher level, where it is freed from the strictures of sense. They are passionate pilgrims of the absolute, restless until they rest in an infinite love that is the intense passion of the Holy Spirit. If they seem to withdraw, it is only for the sake of a fuller life from which the limits of that lower life would have debarred them ... Life is love, passionate and intense. Only in such love is reality touched—the rest is deception, bondage, and spiritual death."*

I wrote down the above quote when listening to a lecture by a spiritual mentor of mine, Fr. William McNamara, who was a Carmelite monk, founder of the Spiritual Life Institute in Crestone, Co., and Silgo, Ireland, and author to more than a dozen books.

What he is saying here is that in any moment, when we are true to ourselves, we can rise to the qualitative standards of sainthood, because we will exhibit the qualities of boldness, humility, passion, and love.

To be hungry for God is true wisdom. We will never be content until that hunger is satisfied. Wisdom does not make us full. It fills us with hunger for stillness, peace, goodness, truth, beauty, and union with the living God. Be a man or a woman of wisdom: God-centered, God-filled, God-intoxicated.

We must employ mortification upon our false selves, meaning we must put our false selves to death. Temperance is the virtue developed through mortification. In other words, it is the self-mastery over our senses and intellect, as well as our feelings and will.

Abnegation is self-denial in order to be of service to others. Abnegation develops humility through sacrifice. John the Baptist said, "He must increase, I must decrease." (John

3:30). I am but a voice, Jesus is the word echoing through all eternity. Abnegation leads to self-transcendence—that is, focusing on the one thing necessary. True abnegation makes us fearless.

Near the end of his life, Pope John XXIII was asked by a reporter, "Holy Father, how can you be so serene, knowing that the end is near?" To which he replied, "My friend, today is a good day. In fact, every day is a good day; a good day to live, and a good day to die."[29]

❧ II ☙
CONVERSION

The Carmelite Order has a wonderful tradition of removing the corpus of Jesus from the cross and places the Latin phrases *Pati Divina* on the vertical beam and *Pati Humani* on the horizontal beam. These inscriptions ask us to open our arms to embrace all that is human vulnerability so as to suffer all that is divine. It is a mystery to be sure.

In Jesus's time, Jewish life was loaded heavily with laws (613 to be exact), which were unified by the double commandment to love:

> *"You should love the Lord your God with all your heart, soul, mind, and strength and your neighbor as yourself."*

This double commandment was a combination of Deuteronomy 6:4-9 and Leviticus 19:18. It also reflected the two tablets of the Ten Commandments—the first three commanding love of God and the last seven commanding love of neighbor.

When Jesus asked the scholar of the law to quote it, the lawyer easily recited this double commandment. In fact, reading his ego between the lines, he could not resist the chance to show off his knowledge and expertise.

At this stage in the story, the lawyer can read the law, but does not know how to live it. He has conceptual knowledge, but lacks the realized understanding that leads to action.

Although the lawyer may see his exchange with Jesus as a battle of wits, Jesus, the Master Teacher, I, crafting His responses in service of the lawyer's request, is guiding the lawyer to live the double commandment.

There is a role reversal: the lawyer initially desired to test Jesus, not seeking to be taught, but seeking to teach, but Jesus answered a question with a question, and as a result, things did not go as planned. Jesus turned the tables and tested the lawyer! Although the lawyer passed the test admirably, the exchange ended with Jesus giving him a command: "Go and do likewise."

The lawyer persists. His question, "Who is my neighbor?" is meant to lead Jesus into a maze of opinions. The lawyer is seeking clear boundaries.

This point is made evident by the Levite and the priest who saw the robbed and beaten man, but passed him by. If they touched a bleeding and/or dead body, they would become impure. If the man was not a Jew, there was no obligation. Did they even entertain an inner debate about what they had to do or what they were excused from doing? This fine-print thinking is the air that legal minds breathe, and it is the air that suffocates Jesus.

The Samaritan responds with compassion and generosity. He immediately puts into action the double commandment of loving God and neighbor. The Samaritan's God-grounded response to the man in the ditch is not only seen in the fact that he crosses ethnic boundaries, it is also revealed in the remarkable extent of his care. He does not seem to know limits. All of his property, his "strength," is put into action in his deep desire to bring healing. His bandages, oil, wine, animal, money, time, and ability to recruit the innkeeper are freely and abundantly brought to bear in his effort of restoring the man to health.

The last line of the parable hints at the unending boundless care that only God can inspire. "I will pay you whatever is needed." The limitless intent of "whatever is needed" is a crystal-clear indication that the Samaritan is loving his neighbor through the love of God.

There exists a fragile co-existence between breakdown and breakthrough, between vice and virtue. Christian educator, writer, and editor Alta Mae Erb wrote a three-parable entry in her book, *The Christian Nurture of Children*, which outlines the conversion process—particularly of those looking to bring others to know God the Father.[30]

She starts each parable, "I took a child's hand in mine," and progresses the "child's" steps through the conversion process. In the first phase, the teacher or adult in the story describes God as a wrathful, stern, powerful being. This arouses fear in the child. Upon meeting the Father, the child cowers and does not take His hand, leaving the teacher standing between child and Father.

In the second parable, Erb describes the child as one coming into his own in the world. He is growing—curious, yet distracted—as a unique individual. The teacher works diligently to fill the child's mind with all things related to the Father. However, the child is bouncing around like a pinball. This time, when the child comes face-to-face with the Father, he cannot focus and again refuses the hand of the Father. Instead, he passes out from exhaustion.

In the final parable of the trilogy, the teacher approaches the child with gratitude, paying better attention to the child's needs and interests. The child begins to have an interest in the Father, remembering and reciting stories back to his teacher. When the child encounters the Father for the third time, he is in awe of His glory. Now the teacher can pass off the hand of the child fully to the Father, and the child willingly grasps the Father's hand. The teacher is content, having led the child to the Father.

Erb is outlining the path to spiritual maturity. First, we cannot understand the spiritual life, so we may fear it. Next, we are distracted by the many outside forces of the world as we search for our own identities. At times, it seems we cannot be bothered with our spiritual endeavors. Finally, one day, grace takes hold, and we finally recognize the divinity of Father, Son, and Holy Spirit. Grace converts us, enabling us to pass on the gift of spiritual direction to our neighbors.

12

DISCIPLESHIP

There is an old legend that says Jesus, as a carpenter, was known for making the best yokes in Galilee. Imagine an advertisement over the door of Jesus's shop touting the good fit and comfort of His yokes. This would lend authenticity to Jesus's words about His yokes making the burden lighter.

As Lawrence O. Richards writes in his commentary, "Being yoked to Jesus doesn't mean so much that we take on His burdens, but that He, pulling alongside us, takes on ours. Yes, it's tough being a disciple ... Yet the disciple, by the very fact of his commitment, is yoked to Jesus. And in that relationship, with Jesus taking on most of the load, we find, not added burdens, but an amazing inner rest."[31]

So, the choice is ours: to live in sin or synergy. To live purposeless lives apart from God or to be yoked to Christ, allowing us to live purposeful, powerful lives.

> *"Take My yoke upon you, and learn from Me, for I am meek and humble of heart; and you will find rest for yourselves. For My yoke is easy, and My burden light."*
> –Matthew 11:29-30

Walking along that path—the spiritual life—consists of five unskippable steps. The first step is to be alert, attentive, vigilant, on-guard.

The second is to be receptive to all of the abundant graces God pours upon us. Mary, the mother of God and our mother, is the best example of being receptive to God's grace. It is also important to remember a basic theological principle here: grace builds on nature. The more natural we are, the more receptive we will be to God's divine life and love.

The third step is to be converted. Fidelity to the mysteries of the rosary enables us to see God in the joy of a child's excitement; to see God in the loved one who is ravaged by cancer; to see God in the glory of enemies becoming friends.

The fourth step is to allow the sacrament of baptism to instill in us a true identity as children of God. It is to allow the Eucharist to nurture us in expressing intimacy in a fully human, wholesome, chaste manner. It is to allow the sacrament of confirmation to strengthen us in integrity. The gifts and the fruits of the Holy Spirit erupt and enable us to be victorious over capital sins and all the petty venial sins that try to trick us every day.

We cannot ignore the residual effects of Original Sin that linger in our souls. These effects are a weakening of the will, a disordering of our emotions, a limiting of our senses, and a warping in our thinking.

In examining our conscience, not only should we examine the morality of our days, but also the quality of our days.

- How human was I?
- How mindful was I?
- How deliberate was I?
- How focused was I?
- How leisurely did I live today?
- How many times did I laugh today?

"To sin is human" is a false truth. Every time we sin, we are less than fully human, and God asks each of us simply to be human. Every decision we face and every reaction we must choose is influenced by the strength of our discipleship. Jesus challenged His apostles' faith frequently.

When Jesus rebukes the boy possessed by a demon, His disciples cannot fathom why they could not do the same thing when asked by the boy's father. "He said to them, 'Because of your little faith. Amen, I say to you, if you have faith the size of a mustard seed, you will say to this mountain, 'Move from here to there,' and it will move. Nothing will be impossible for you." (Matthew 17:20).

The issue of faith as an important basis for miracles is raised in His hometown, where He "was not able to perform any mighty deed there, apart from curing a few sick people by laying his hands on them. He was amazed at their lack of faith." (Mark 6:5-6).

Christ could have turned the stones into bread at the devil's behest, but He did not because it would have been a violation of the testing which He had been led by the Spirit to endure. Therefore, He generally performed miracles on behalf of those who were willing to trust in Him.

Jesus rebukes His disciples for their *oligopistia*, or "little faith." Faith can grow, like a mustard seed, from something very small into something quite large. Sometimes it is fickle and not solid, never taking root, quickly dying off, or choked by weeds. Sometimes it is limited by fear. Sometimes it can apparently be genuine but then quickly turn from acceptance to rejection. Many of those who had some faith in Jesus eventually turned their backs on Him.

When Jesus went to Tyre and Sidon, he was approached by a bold, courageous, and persistent Canaanite woman. Her love for her daughter was so great that she was willing to overcome every obstacle placed in her way in order to liberate the child from the possession of a demon.

Jesus's first response to her request was stone silence. Secondly, she had to overcome the recommendation of the disciples to send this whiny woman away. Third, she was not part of the "in crowd," as Jesus alludes to the idea that He was sent "only to the lost sheep of the house of Israel." (Matthew 15:24). Fourth, she had to endure a cruel insult. "It is not right to take the food of the children and throw it to the dogs." (Matthew 15:25). This feisty woman turned the insult inside out and upside down. She cleverly responded, "Please Lord, even the dogs eat the scraps that fall from their masters' tables." (Matthew 15:27).

Jesus recognizes this woman's great faith and heals her daughter. Jesus challenges us all to believe, with unwavering vigor, that all things are possible in His name. It is our responsibility as spiritually mature people to remain attentive to our daily experiences and the impulse of the Holy Spirit.

The 5 Unskippable Steps

1. Mindfulness – Be awake. Be attentive. Be alert. Be on guard. Be vigilant
2. Receptivity – Be receptive to the spiritual gifts and spiritual fruits of the Holy Spirit and the abundant graces for every situation and circumstance
3. Conversion – Pick up your cross daily and follow in His footsteps
4. Discipleship – Come be a lifelong student of Jesus. Come and listen. Come and learn. Come and gather your strength. Come and be nourished at the table of the Lord
5. Apostleship – Go in the name of Jesus. Go and teach. Go and heal. Go and proclaim the Good News. Go and baptize

IV
THE EASTER SEASON

Easter is the feast of feasts. It is a time for fresh water rather than blood; for flowers rather than nails; for peace in place of pain; for open fields rather than the hill of the skull. Easter heals Calvary and reveals what happens when hope is steadfast unto death. How we all need the healing hope of Easter!

Jesus is our new dawn ... our new light. Jesus is our hope in the victory over sin and death.

Easter is the very heart of our faith. Resurrection involves us in a complete transformation of life. In each of us lives the dearest, freshest, deep-down things. Despite hardship, despite suffering, despite sin, despite death, He is risen. Jesus is alive. He came to share new life with us. The fruits of the new life are light, peace, joy, and hope. The dry, barren desert of Lent gives way to the fertile, flowing water of Easter.

The paschal imprint we celebrate is that of death and resurrection. Without death, resurrection becomes a completely meaningless term. Without resurrection, death becomes hopeless.

Easter never tires of reminding us that we are loved. We

were passionately, intimately, wildly, madly loved long before our parents, family members, friends, teachers, and spouses loved us or wounded us. That is the truth of our lives. To live our lives out of the awareness that we are so beloved is to say that God's love is unconditional and has the power to overcome sin and death itself.

C.S. Lewis said, "If you read history you will find that the Christians begin the most for the present world are just the ones that thought the most of the next. The Apostles themselves, who set on foot in the conversion of the Roman Empire, the great men who built up the Middle Ages, the English Evangelicals who abolished the Slave Trade, all left their mark one Earth, precisely because their minds were occupied with Heaven. It is since Christians have largely ceased to think of the other world that they have become so in effective in this. And that Heaven and you'll get the earth 'thrown in': aim at earth and you'll get neither."[32]

In the breaking of the bread, the disciples not only see a change in Jesus, they come to see the whole world as changed —radically transformed.

The Christian view of the world can be reduced to a simple formula:

1. The world is good
2. The world is fallen
3. The world will be redeemed

As I reflect on life experiences, I recognize a common pattern: what begins with a burst of excitement often settles into familiarity and ends in disappointment. For example, falling in love, bringing home a newborn from the hospital, a child's first day of school, the thrill of learning to read. These are all hallmark events in our lives so vivid with promise at the time, yet all too often, they eventually lose their luster.

How can you keep that initial excitement from fading into familiarity and finally souring as disappointment?

The Blessed Trinity's graceful giving has the last word. Paradoxically, life is found in death. Less paradoxically, life is found in a love that holds on through death. Our knowledge of the unity of the cross and resurrection does not remove the darkness of the cross. Although we can talk about it from the outside, the passing over remains a mystery that we must live.

We have no choice about physical death, but the other dying is up to us: we decide whether we will die with Jesus. We are not doomed by our circumstances. The choice is ours. Will we live from our heart with Jesus, pouring ourselves out in love? Or will we shield ourselves from the world's pain in fear and self-protection?

Frequently when I visit a person in a nursing home who is in a desperate condition, I am amazed by the faith and peace that come from that person's smiling eyes. Love pours forth from the dying of Jesus within. I recall Hemingway's description of the fisherman, Santiago. "Everything about him was old except his eyes. They were the same color as the sea and were cheerful and undefeated."[33]

As the interior death grows, resurrection life also grows. Death and life are intertwined. St. Paul said this magnificently, "...always carrying about in the body the dying of Jesus, so that the life of Jesus may also be manifested in our body. For we who live are constantly being given up to death for the sake of Jesus, so that the life of Jesus may be manifested in our mortal flesh." (2 Corinthians 4:10-11).

The word for "death" here is used only twice in the New Testament—both times by St. Paul—and it carries the nuance of "dying." We carry about in our living bodies the dying of Jesus.

The 4H Club

HUMILITY

HILARITY

HOSPITALITY

HOLINESS

13

DISCERNMENT

Each of us needs to discover and declare our life's "game plan." Any athlete or coach can understand the importance of game planning and the art of being attentive to how a game is unfolding in real time in order to make the necessary adjustments.

That is what is known as discernment. While it is essential in many aspects of our lives, it is vital to a life of spiritual maturity.

Spiritually speaking, discernment is an art, a science and a charism. In many ways, discernment is simple:

- Is this thought from the Evil Spirit?
- Is this thought from the Ego Spirit?
- Is this thought from the Holy Spirit?

The game plan for each of us is different, but these five facets are involved for us all: physical, emotional, intellectual, social and spiritual. How we allow stress to impact that game plan can make a significant difference in experiencing the abundant life Jesus came to bring us.

How do we create a game plan for the spiritual life? A

daily examination of conscience. By our own attentiveness to our actions we will come to recognize our motivations and be able to pinpoint what's going right and what's going wrong. We shall become aware of the relationship between our actions and our feelings.

Have you been watching more television than normal this week? How did you come to that conclusion? Is it because you've been feeling a bit of an emotional emptiness lately?

Do you feel your pants hugging your waistline a bit tighter this month? Perhaps you've been mindlessly eating more comfort food or have tossed your exercise regimen to the side, because you've been spending longer hours at the office.

Did you become intellectually lazy during a rest-filled time? Has your reading suffered as a result? Did you find yourself feeling socially imprisoned socially during the pandemic of 2020? Did you feel your freedom was challenged?

Finally, have you abandoned daily prayer?

These five aspects of our spiritual game plan are inherently connected; neglecting one or two of them will have negative consequences on the other three. If your prayer life, social life, emotional life and reading habits to develop our mind are attended to, it's a good bet that attentiveness to diet or sleep will follow suit.

Having to balance five areas of life may seem overwhelming. What is required? The simple consistent practice of mindful repetition.

If you want to mature in the spiritual life, daily prayer is where you begin. Abraham Joshua Heschel gives us a clue of what mature prayer is:

"Prayer requires education, training, reflection, contemplation. It is not enough to join others; it is necessary to build a sanctuary within, brick by brick, instants of meditation, moments of devotion."[34]

We do *not* pray in order to discover answers. We pray in order to allow His kingdom and His will to have greater influence in the way we think, speak, and act. The goal of prayer is not personal fulfillment. We pray to create inner space for greater divine influence. We do not pray in the hope to assure a desired outcome or to gain some kind of mystical insight into life. No, we pray in order to surrender to His way, His truth, His life. We pray to become more aware that we are beloved sons and daughters of the Blessed Trinity.

Thomas Merton compared the spiritual life to a search for a path in a field of untrodden snow: "Walk across the snow and there is your path."[35]

Prayer is also a time to *listen*. Listen to the Father, Son, and Holy Spirit as they speak words of life and love to you, to me, to everyone willing to listen. Their language is clear and simple.

- I made you in my image after my likeness. God saw all He had made and indeed it was very good. (as told in Genesis 1:26, 31)
- I raise you up to my cheeks. (as told in Hosea 11:4)
- "I call you by name." (Isaiah 43:1)
- "I hold you in the palm of my hand." (as told in Isaiah 49:16)
- "I have established a new covenant with you, a heartfelt covenant. I have written the law of love upon your heart." (as told in Jeremiah 31:31-34)
- "You are my beloved Son; with you I am well pleased." (Mark 1:11)
- "Put on then, as God's chosen ones, holy and beloved..." (Colossians 3:12)

Our experience of centering/listening prayer will transform us slowly. Gradually, it will equip us to face stress, tension, anxiety, tension—all the challenges of daily living that beset us.

Prayer strengthens us to live life with courage, confidence and peace. Prayer is all about love—both human and divine.

There is little spiritual benefit in praying mindlessly. Jesus was reluctant to teach his disciples to pray with a set formula. He wanted the fisherman, the tax collector, His inner circle to learn a methodology of prayer instead of memorizing prayers.

We must commit to praying every day. We begin by being attentive to what's going on inside us. Little by little, we recognize some impulse as coming from the Holy Spirit, and through a growing receptivity, we learn the art of how the Holy Spirit leads us in our present circumstances. Our lives change significantly as a result.

If we remain attentive to the guidance of the Holy Spirit, it will be like watching a gentle stream. We see it flowing underneath the pebbles or the moss. It is calming. Its movement connects with our inner movement. By receiving slight nudges of the Holy Spirit day in and day out, we develop a wider perspective.

"And suddenly there came from the sky a noise like a strong driving wind..." (Acts 2:2). The Holy Spirit blows, like the wind, where it may. The opening line of Nikos Kazantzakis's *The Last Temptation of Christ* states, "A cool heavenly breeze took possession of him."[36] That's a profoundly creative way of saying the Holy Spirit descended upon him, lifted him up, and moved him toward where he needed to go.

When the spiritually mature person remains attentive to his or her ability to discern, he or she is allowing the Holy Spirit to exhibit the grace of guidance and direction in all areas of life—physically, intellectually, emotionally, socially, and spiritually.

14
HUMILITY

There are things to be learned from sin—compassion, empathy, perception, and humility. Without the ability to own our own sins, these qualities are all hard to come by indeed. Unless we accept our incompleteness, we can never grow from it. Whatever the heights of our present virtue, the bottomless pit of life stretches always before us, always to be respected, always in the throes of challenging us to look at ourselves again.

Humility reminds us that we are all in process always, and to be in process is perfectly all right. As the proverb says, "It is not where we are that counts. It is where we are going that matters."

Detachment does not mean that we love nothing but God; it means that we love all in God. It does not mean we learn to love creatures less and less; it means that we learn to love them more and more—but selflessly—as part of our vast undivided love of God. To enjoy any living thing: fire, water, air, animal, vegetable, human, even God Himself, we must let go of it.

It requires a lot of inner solitude and silence to become aware of the gentle movements of the spirit of God. He does not shout, scream, or push. The spirit of God is soft and gentle like a whispering voice or a light breeze.

The way of Jesus is the way of downward mobility. It is the way toward the poor, the suffering, the marginal, the prisoners, the refugees, the lonely, the hungry, the dying, the tortured, the homeless—toward all who ask for compassion. What do they have to offer? Not success, popularity, or power, but the joy and peace of being children of God.

Charity is the central virtue of life. Faith is the foundational virtue. Humility is the indispensable virtue. Reverence is the key virtue.

Spiritual direction is another form of downward mobility and it has been an incredible gift and blessing in my life. It is a necessary part of spiritual growth. It is very obvious to me that the Holy Spirit was at work in leading me to my spiritual director, Dan Murray. He, in his great humility and docility, was a huge instrument in my life, as God allowed the Holy Spirit to work through him. The Lord placed him in my life to help show me the way. It is obvious that his wisdom and ability to guide me was a fruit of his prayer for me and of a genuine desire to know and understand me. I greatly appreciated his careful balance of patience, gentleness, boldness, and positive pressure. I needed to be pushed and held accountable for the changes that needed to be made in my life.

The meetings I had with my spiritual director taught me practical ways to change my way of thinking about myself, the Lord, and different struggles that I was dealing with at the time. When I found myself in a rut, feeling that I was unable to move forward, spiritual direction helped me develop a new game plan.

A receiver of spiritual direction should pray for his or her spiritual director and come prepared to share life's struggles and lingering questions of the soul.

Regular confession helps to recognize patterns of sin in our lives. Spiritual direction is a place of safety and trust. A beautiful fruit of my confessions and sharing my struggles is knowing that I am seen in all my imperfections and brokenness and still loved. My spiritual director wanted me to know above all, that I am a son of the Blessed Trinity, that I am profoundly, passionately, and perfectly loved by Father, Son, and Holy Spirit.

Spiritual direction has been a place where I have seen and experienced the love of Christ. It has been a source of great freedom and openness to the Lord's will in my life.

My time as a spiritual director for others is a great fruit, too. The Lord has given me opportunities—more than forty-years' worth—to share with others what Dan Murray showed me in and through spiritual direction. I proudly pass along the wisdom that my spiritual director offered me in honor of the life he lived on Earth.

To show gratitude and be able to speak to the influence someone played on your life is a great practice of humility. I can think of no better example than the Heisman Trophy acceptance speech by John Cappelletti.

I knew the Cappelletti family as I was John's classmate at Monsignor Bonner High School in Drexel Hill. When the news struck that his younger brother, Joey, was diagnosed with leukemia at age five, the community was hit hard.

Joey survived six years before experiencing his brother dedicating the most coveted award in college sports to him. He tragically passed away two years later.

Famed sports columnist Bill Lyon recapped the speech in *The Philadelphia Inquirer* on Dec. 14, 1973. "He never complains, he never asks why; he accepts it but he refuses to give up," John Cappelletti said. "He's been through so much that it makes me feel what I go through – and then the rewards I get in return – well, it's all so small compared to him, and ..."[37]

Not able to hold his tears back, John simply uttered to the people in attendance, "Joey has been an inspiration for me."[38]

Lyon poetically concluded his recounting of that special night with what I can only describe as the grace of spiritual maturity in a nutshell:

"When John Cappelletti sat down there were a lot of wet eyes and the applause lasted a long, long time. The people realized they had seen something very special. Something bigger than any trophy ever made. It's called love."[39]

To be immersed in a moment like that is humility. You are giving up all of the chatter in your mind—we've got to put the kids to bed when we get home, I still have work to finish up, I could really go for another cocktail right about now—and making space for something greater than you.

15
HILARITY

Jesus portrays an attitude and style that mixes cheerfulness, merriment, and good humor. Romans dubbed this virtue *hilaritas*.[40] It is a joyful confidence, an affirmation of life even in the face of diminishment. It is the celebration of the supper before betrayal and crucifixion; the insistence of the kingdom of another world, while in chains before the king of this world; the talk of paradise while nailed to the tree of rejection.

Hilaritas is a freedom that does not allow the circumstances of life to dictate moods and feelings. This idea runs through Jesus's rejection of worry in Matthew 6:25-34.

> "Therefore I tell you, do not worry about your life, what you will eat, or about your body, what you will wear. Is not life more than food and the body more than clothing? Look at the birds in the sky; they do not sow or reap, they gather nothing into barns, yet your heavenly Father feeds them. Are not you more important than they? Can any of you by worrying add a single moment to your life-span? Why are you anxious about clothes? Learn from the way the wild flowers grow. They do not work or spin. But I tell you that

not even Solomon in all his splendor was clothed like one of them. If God so clothes the grass of the field, which grows today and is thrown into the oven tomorrow, will he not much more provide for you, O you of little faith? So do not worry and say, 'What are we to eat?' or 'What are we to drink?' or 'What are we to wear?' All these things the pagans seek. Your heavenly Father knows that you need them all. But seek first the kingdom [of God] and his righteousness, and all these things will be given you besides. Do not worry about tomorrow; tomorrow will take care of itself. Sufficient for a day is its own evil."

This enduringly beautiful passage is Hilaritas's playful reminder not to let worry be the whole story about life.

Hilaritas is not frivolity nor flightiness. Hilaritas is passionately involved with the pain of the world, but not absorbed by it. Hilaritas takes life seriously but not ultimately. It strives for betterment, yet at the moment of disaster it may wink. Hilaritas understands human growth occurs for the most part by inches. You take three steps forward and two steps backward, but still reach your goal.

Hilaritas has the courage to surprise the world with new acts of love. The Master washes the feet of His disciples; a Samaritan helps a Jew; a Jew shares faith and a meal with a gentile. Hilaritas is acceptance and transcendence.

William James says laughter is always a religious experience.[41] Angels move quickly because they take themselves lightly. The most neglected line in the gospels is the injunction from Matthew, "...do not look gloomy..." (Matthew 6:16).

An ancient custom of the Greek Orthodox Church reserves the day after Easter for laughter and hilarity. On this day, the sanctuary is filled with festivity and joking to celebrate the cosmic joke God pulled on Satan in the resurrection —the source of Christian joy and celebration, the music to which we ceaselessly dance, the Son which we forever sing.

16

HOSPITALITY

"Love the poor and your life will be filled with sunlight and you will not be frightened at the moment of death."
—St. Vincent de Paul

The shortest distance between a human being and truth is a story. Stories are healing to our spirits, enriching to our imaginations. As disciples of the Lord, it is vitally important to know the story of Jesus, to know the story of the church—saints, martyrs, and sinners. May God give us the grace throughout our lives to connect our story with the story of Jesus and the communion of saints.

In Genesis 18, Abraham and Sarah show hospitality to three strangers who came to them by the oaks of Mamre and the Lord rewards them with a son, despite their old age and Sarah's biological inability to further have children.

In the second book of Kings, the prophet Elisha was extended hospitality by an unnamed woman of influence.

She says to her husband, "I know that he is a holy man of God. Since he visits us often, let us arrange a little room on the roof and furnish it for him with a bed, table, chair, and lamp, so that when he comes to us he can stay there." (2 Kings 4:9-10).

When he did, he was ever grateful for her hospitality. The woman had no son and her husband was old, yet one year later, she gave birth to a son and the child grew up healthy.

Jesus told the parable of the prodigal son in Luke 15. The son's father was extremely insulted by him because he was asking for half of his inheritance before his father died. He displayed incredible spiritual immaturity and went out and lived a profligate life—wine, women, and song.

Then came to a moment of awareness. What did he do? He rehearsed his apology.

"Father, I have sinned against heaven and against you. I no longer deserve to be called your son; treat me as you would treat one of your hired workers." (Luke 15:18-19).

Meanwhile, the father looked out every night to see if his son was on the horizon, and eventually, he saw his son. He recognized his son from a distance and ran to him. In the culture of the New Testament, a father running like that was inappropriate behavior, but he's now representing our Heavenly Father. When we sin, we think we're distant and an outcast. Au contraire! Father, Son, and Holy Spirit are going to wait for us and wait for the opportunity to run toward us and bring us back. What happened? He has no shoes, and he receives sandals for his feet. He has no ring, and he gets a ring on his finger. He's showered with sonship. He gets a new garment and a feast!

The 4H club—Humility, Hilarity, Hospitality, Holiness—is a place where no one stands separate from the other. Each one is a stepping stone for the next. We need humility to welcome hilarity. We need hilarity to be hospitable. We become holy when we are consistently hospitable. These are the foundations to enrichment.

A hospitable person makes people feel welcome. That very notion heals others. Any time the word "healing" shows up in the bible, hospitality is not far ahead or behind. Any time forgiveness is mentioned in the bible, hospitality is there, hand in hand. Any time salvation or feeling love comes into play, what do you think caused that feeling in the first place? Hospitality.

Most people don't want to buy damaged goods. Yet, redemption is one of the keys to eternal life and hospitality is the keyring. Without a doubt, the antidote to hostility in the world in hospitality.

The little boy in John 6 who offers five barley loaves and two fish showed great hospitality to the village. Barley loaves are the bread of the poor, but who does he offer them to? Jesus, who turns around, blesses them, has the disciples break the bread and distribute it to 10,000 people.

The little boy in John 6 who offers five barley loaves and two fish showed great hospitality to the gathered crowd. Barley loaves are the bread of the poor and to whom does the lad offer them? Jesus! He takes and blesses them. Has his disciples break and distribute them and feeds 10,000 people! More astonishingly, after all are satisfied, Jesus has the disciples pick up whatever remains – 12 basketsful! Now that's hospitality!

When we risk giving to the Lord, we receive in abundance. Those who tithe know this. It is a big risk, giving ten percent of all we earn. But those who do tend nearly always to feel they receive back one-hundred-fold. Their generosity is outdone by God's.

It takes spiritual maturity to believe such can happen; when it does it is glorious!

A person who is inhospitable is a miser on all levels of life. A spiritually immature person does not trust taking risks with his or her hard-earned money, his or her precious time, or his or her false sense of reputation. Clear and simple.

17

HOLINESS

Religious traditions across the world have recognized the importance of abandonment as an unskippable step in spiritual maturity. Every disciple of Jesus is called to abandon an inordinate desire for security—for youthful appearance and uninterrupted good health, for material possessions, or for an intact reputation. These desires are not bad, but to covet them as if they could bring us serenity and complete contentment on Earth is to entertain self-deception and a glaring lack of self-awareness.

As Pope Francis said, we welcome the risen Jesus as a friend, with trust.

"He is life!" he wrote. "He will receive you with open arms. If you have been indifferent, take a risk: you won't be disappointed. If following him seems difficult, don't be afraid, trust him, be confident that he is close to you, he is with you and he will give you the peace you are looking for and the strength to live as he would have you do."[42]

A spiritually mature person accepts the fruits and gifts of the Holy Spirit with open arms. The gift of the Holy Spirit is the "living water" of contemplation. The fruits of contemplation are to be possessed by the truth, consumed by love, overwhelmed by beauty, and passionately attached to the good.

Jesus gave us the formula for sharing in His Father's life in the Beatitudes. At first, they seem contradictory. On closer inspection, they seem radical. When compared to everyday life, they seem impossible. Yet, Jesus offers them as attitudes that will make us happy now and for eternity.

He does not equivocate. Any authentic student and disciple—all who know themselves to be children of God—will exhibit these characteristics:

1. **Poor in spirit:** What does it mean? Completely void of possessions? No. The kingdom of God is the first and *the* most important possession, and they could let go of any other possession they have
2. **Sorrowing:** Those disturbed by the lack of enthusiasm for the kingdom of Heaven
3. **Lowly, meek:** Individuals who get excited about doing what is right—they never place themselves first
4. **Hunger and thirst:** A right relationship with God is more important than the food and drink they consume
5. **Mercy:** "Love shared," the generous giver, the gracious receiver
6. **Single-hearted:** An uncluttered heart consumed by the kingdom of God
7. **Peacemakers:** They bring fullness of life to other people's lives—the full potential in their husbands, wives, and children
8. **Righteous:** They do not fear persecution for living by the word of the Lord

Living the Beatitudes will undoubtedly disturb those who are complacent, apathetic, and selfish. They magnify in an embarrassing way the false gods many people worship today: productivity, profit, power, pleasure, pettiness, prestige, prettiness, and pride. All of these goals are contrary to the values inherent in the Beatitudes. Superficiality leads us astray. Convention can compel us to be satisfied with the norm. Consumerism is "selfishness with large."

The future may be uncertain. We will meet and overcome many roadblocks on the road to holiness. Persecution and ridicule may befall any authentic follower of Jesus. Nevertheless, we have Jesus's solemn promise that those who incarnate these Christ-like virtues will be numbered among the saints.

The Beatitudes are an autobiography. We prove that we are people who long to see the face of God by making the eight Beatitudes the foundation of our spiritual lives. Such virtuous living is contagious. As we begin to transform ourselves, we begin to transform the society in which we live!

Love of God and love of neighbor are the irrefutable guiding commandments for all followers of Christ. Countless holy people have illuminated our way. Some have gone before us marked with the sign of faith. Whether or not their names are known, we commemorate and celebrate that "great multitude, which no one could count." (Revelation 7:9).

St. Paul used the word "saint" as a synonym for every member of the early Christian community. Holiness or sainthood does not have to involve an elaborate canonization ceremony. The Gospel informs us that saints are those who, every day, try to purify their hearts, hunger and thirst for God's ways, are peacemakers, risk being poor in spirit, are vulnerable to the sorrows of everyday living, and try to be merciful.

The Beatitudes bring happiness and blessing to those who embrace them. Given the present-day standards of the world, it sounds a bit strange to think that real happiness entails grieving, practicing non-violence, and a willingness to be marginalized. Nevertheless, the Beatitudes constitute Jesus's platform for entrance into God's kingdom.

18
NEW LIFE

Two weeks before Easter Sunday, the Liturgy bids us to reflect on death and life. Lent is a time for soul searching and spiritual house cleaning. Death faces us in the story of Lazarus. The sobering lesson is that being a friend of Jesus did not protect us from pain and suffering or from heartbreaking experiences.

Just consider Martha and Mary. They thought of Jesus as the miracle worker. He had raised Jairus's daughter from the dead, but He did not come to them in their hour of need. They were angry because Jesus did not seem to care enough to come when they sent for Him; when their brother Lazarus was still alive, while there was still some hope.

But Jesus had a plan. His purpose in delaying was to show the mighty power God has over death. Jesus grieved and wept over the death of His friend. He mourned this loss and then consoled Martha and Mary, assuring them that death is not the final word. He then restored Lazarus to life with the words: "Lazarus, come forth!"

This Gospel is also about life. It addresses the longing all of us have for receiving life in the face of death or meaningless existence.

The prophet Ezekiel is famous for the image of a valley of dry bones—a windswept battlefield where soldiers once engaged in mortal conflict. All that is left are the skeletal remains of those who have fallen in battle.

Lives are sometimes like that. Lives get broken. Friendships die and wither. Unrealized dreams of youth fade away. Marriages break apart. Children are abused. Nations wage war. People spend their lives feverishly trying to get to the top of the ladder. They are burned out, fed up, done in, stressed out, and overwhelmed. Who will bring new life to this valley of dead bones?

What are left are shells of broken people with broken hearts, broken dreams, and broken promises. However, just as Ezekiel's vision sees the dry bones coming to life, so, too, we can come to new life in Christ, through the spirit of Christ living in all us.

How? We have to hear Jesus call us forth from the tombs we have made for ourselves by:

1. Letting go of a tenaciously held idea, which we know is wrong and inappropriate
2. Relinquishing what we know is an impossible dream
3. Allowing a child to become an adult
4. Leaving unsaid a wounding remark
5. Knowing desolation is an inevitable part of life, which will eventually give way to consolation

Every time we let go of these dry bones and tomblike times, we turn our lives around. We come out of those tombs with a new lease on life. We are converted.

Granted, raising Lazarus was only a glimpse, a dress rehearsal for the real raising to life, which is not just a resuscitation, but radical resurrection. This was a preview of the biggest coming attraction of all: when we experience what God has prepared for everyone who loves Him.

The resurrection of Jesus is the crowning truth of our faith and signifies new life. At the heart of our Christian identity is the belief that our Heavenly Father has radically changed the universe in the birth, life, passion, death, and resurrection of Jesus.

Resurrection is the focus of our Easter season—the "great fifty days." Easter is so important that we cannot celebrate it adequately in one day. It takes a week of weeks. The season's spirituality is shaped by the Acts of the Apostles. Each day at mass, both Sundays and weekdays, we discover anew our Christian identity.

The new life we experience after Jesus's ministry ends on Earth and the apostles begin to spread the Gospel is one that is meant to be unified. The Acts of the Apostles explains in detail the transition from Peter sharing the word of the Lord primarily with Jews in Jerusalem and Samaria to Paul traveling across the Roman Empire to make known the Good News to the gentiles.

These very acts display God's intent that all people share equally in the hope and salvation of His kingdom.

The paschal mystery realized dying to the old, abandoning old ways. This is required so the new life of victory over sin and death can flourish. It is now that the church begins taking on its identity.

It was not easy for the apostles to step out of their comfort zones and journey into the world of the gentiles. Conversion was essential to face the challenges in this unfamiliar territory.

In Acts, the apostles are no longer spiritually immature. The contrast is stark. Those same apostles who had "little faith" and great fear have been given new life through the fruits and gifts of the Holy Spirit.

It is when we let go of control that we too can experience

this new life—this new understanding of our spiritual journey and our role in God's divine master plan.

Bernard Lonergan, a Canadian Jesuit priest, philosopher, and theologian, supported this eloquently in his study of human understanding: "Without any experience of just how and why, one is in the state of grace or one recovers it, one leaves all things to follow Christ, one binds oneself by vows of poverty, chastity and obedience, one gets through one's daily heavy dose of prayer."[43]

His breadth and depth of human understanding evidences itself in his further explanation that when we are so immersed in divine love, we have no choice but to feel a burning desire to express human love. Our concerns, interests, hopes, and dreams are engulfed in "nature and grace," and our new understanding of the Gospel allows us to have life and live it abundantly.

When we have experienced new life at this level of our spiritual maturity, we are no longer bothered by fear, worry, angst, or dissatisfaction. We know His way guides us.

Lonergan describes it as an unconscious act of intense divine love rather than a thought or a feeling.

The Trappist monk Thomas Merton builds off of this idea, where all things flow when we have found our vocation —our purpose. "Now everything is in unity, in order, at peace. Now work no longer interferes with prayer or prayer with work. Now contemplation no longer needs to be a special 'state' that removes one from the ordinary things going on around him for God penetrates all. One does not have to think of giving an account of oneself to anyone but Him."[44]

The Acts of the Apostles begins with the descent of the Holy Spirit upon the apostles at Pentecost. How fitting it is then that the apostles receive new life and we celebrate the birth of our church with three great feasts following the Easter season.

V
THE THREE GREAT FEASTS

When Jesus takes Peter, James, and John up the mountain in the transfiguration scene they experience ecstasy in the highest order. Peter's excitement to see Elijah and Moses talking to his Master Teacher is paramount. Then, a cloud casts over the group in classic biblical fashion and a voice comes from the sky, "This is my beloved Son. Listen to him." (Mark 9:7). The prophets disappear and the disciples are left alone with Jesus the man, yet again, who leads them in their descent back down the mountain.

In the time period that follows the Easter season—those great fifty days—the church leads us back down the mountain of the highest order: Jesus's resurrection. We celebrate with three feasts.

According to my dear friend and director of the Office for Divine Worship in the Archdiocese of Philadelphia, Reverend Gerald Dennis Gill, "Year after year, we celebrate these three great solemnities—Pentecost, holy Trinity, and *Corpus Christi*, Sunday after Sunday. We might conclude that somehow, they are related to one another or flow from one into the other. In truth, all three of these solemnities have unique and distinct histories behind them."

We begin our descent down the mountain with the celebration of Pentecost, which was the Holy Spirit's descent upon the disciples after Jesus's ascension on the seventh Sunday after Easter. Today, it marks the eighth Sunday of Easter, the conclusion of the fifty days of Easter time, and the completion of the paschal mystery. Rev. Gill continues, "The Solemnity of Pentecost has its roots in the Jewish Feast of Weeks, a joyful period of thanksgiving. In the tradition, it also had its own octave to extend its commemoration."

In imagery reflecting the Blessed Trinity, the Father is always at the top of the triangle; Jesus and the Holy Spirit are the Father's representation on Earth. We celebrate this miracle on the Sunday following Pentecost during the solemnity known as the Most Holy Trinity.

We complete our descent on the following Sunday with the Feast of Corpus Christi—Jesus as the bread of life, which will nourish us and sustain us in Ordinary Time. It is known as the Solemnity of the Most Holy Body and Blood of Christ. This gift of the Eucharist—the source and summit of our Catholic faith and true presence of Christ in His Eucharistic body—nourishes and sustains us in our journey on Earth to our destination of the place prepared for us in Heaven.

Ordinary Time in the church is the indication we need to order the gift of time in a grace-filled way. The three feasts and the great fifty days are *extraordinary* time in liturgical life and in the rhythm of the church.

There are "Five Puny C's" we must avoid in order progress into Ordinary Time with awareness and attentiveness rather than blindly or chaotically. They are control, compulsion, competition, consumption, and comparison.

The spiritually immature way is the unwavering need to be in charge of every little detail. It is obsession with things "out of control." Spiritual immaturity can lead to hurting others because of an egotistical desire to be better than the rest. It is consumerism at the highest measure. Most dangerously, it is in conformity or a jealous tendency to want to be something other than our true selves.

How do we defeat these Five Puny C's? With spiritual maturity and the "One Big C" of the Gospel—contemplation. The Gospel invites us to offset the corrosive effects of the Five Puny C's by praying, eating, driving, working, and living contemplatively.

A spiritually mature person humbly wants more enrichment from the peace, joy, kindness, goodness, and generosity of the Holy Spirit, and is attentive to the actions of the Holy Spirit, which minimizes control, compulsion, competition, consumption, and comparison.

I challenge you, when making the sign of the cross, to immerse yourself with everything you know about The Father, and the Son, and the Holy Spirit. Do not simply perform the gesture mindlessly, as many do. Open up your mind and think about your relationship with the Heavenly Father. Open up yourself to a new experience in the heartfelt love of Jesus Christ. Remember and embrace the fruits and gifts of the Holy Spirit. Find strength in them. Tap into them. There is nothing anyone can throw at you that you cannot handle with this power.

The 5 Puny C's

CONTROL

COMPULSION

COMPETITION

CONSUMPTION

COMPARISON

The 1 Big C of the Gospel

CONTEMPLATION

19

IDENTITY

At the time of this writing, ten of my friends died over the course of several weeks. A priest is no stranger to death. As pastor at my present assignment at St. Matthew's Parish in Conshohocken, Pa., I celebrate funeral liturgies with considerable regularity: on average, three per week. However, I cannot remember handling so many deaths in so short a span of time.

No person is so old that he or she does not think another year of life is possible. We accept our own mortality in theory, but we approach each day as if we expect to live indefinitely.

Far from allowing death to heighten the significance of our daily experiences, we, for the most part, work hard to distance ourselves from it. I realize more than ever that death casts a backward shadow on our present moment.

For many people death renders life meaningless.

Samuel Beckett, an Irish playwright, said, "Life is a confusing journey toward oblivion." We fear death, we fear that it makes life absurd, and we flee from death at almost every opportunity. Death can easily impart a bleak futility to life. We recoil from death because it brings isolation and separation.

Without ***faith*** in the resurrection, without ***memories*** that are living in the present, without ***love***—human and divine—death is a merciless foe.

Life is fragile. Death is painful. Funerals and gravesides are places to acknowledge our weakness and our common mortality.

> *"Despite everything, life is full of beauty and meaning. We have been marked by suffering for a whole lifetime. And yet life in its unfathomable depths is so wonderfully good."*
> *–Etty Hillesum*[45]

On the other side of death is new meaning in life, which is why it is so important for each individual follower of Christ to carve out his or her own identity in the grand plan of salvation history. Our entire identities are based on performing a role. We must decide if it is a role completely dictated by others—a false sense of self.

Do you perform to please others, win acceptance, and/or move up the ladder? If so, you are not internalizing your own values or belief system.

When emptiness sets in or a role cannot be fulfilled, the result is identity crisis—more clearly defined as hollowness. Resentment for the very people we originally wanted to serve, begins to take over, and the phrase "you become what you hate" sets in.

If our own fulfillment centers around this type of role identification, we are at severe danger of suffering from burnout. However, that could be the most opportune moment. It is the moment we become enlightened and are forced by the circumstances of our own doing to reevaluate our previous values, beliefs, and ideals.

The spiritually mature person solves this identity crisis not by identifying with a role, but orienting to one. With role orientation, there is a sense of personal spiritual identity in

Christ—the internalization of Christian values and virtues—before a particular role is accepted. We commit to the evangelical virtues of poverty, chastity, and obedience and identity is rooted in Christ independent of the approval of others.

Our interests outside a particular role allow us to find balance, meet new people, and be refreshed.

The feast of Pentecost celebrates not only the birth of the church, but the birth of the *identity* of the church. This birth took place in an upstairs room of a house in Jerusalem. Jesus's initial work in our redemption was done. He ascended to heaven to join His Father once more. But the public ministry, the passion, death, resurrection, and ascension were not the end of Jesus's work. It was only the beginning of a very long process, and that's why He sent the Holy Spirit on the first Pentecost. The Holy Spirit would guide, teach, and sanctify the church until Jesus came again.

The story of Babel in the book of Genesis is a foil to Pentecost. Pentecost reverses the Babel story: jealousy, suspicion, bitterness, resentment, isolation gives way to a whole new language of excitement, joy, hope, forgiveness, kindness, patience, humility, unity, and love. People are intoxicated with the Holy Spirit. But not everybody who heard the apostles' testimony that day was touched by it. In the crowd that day there were three kinds of people: spectators, scoffers, and those who were Spirit-filled.

Three thousand people were added to the Church but Jerusalem was filled with more than 100,000 people for the feast. Many of them paused outside the house where a strong wind was heard, yet they moved on. They were attracted by the spectacle but were not moved by the Spirit. The church still has a lot of spectators. They are not ready to move into action. They might dip their toes into the water but will never take the plunge.

Pentecost and the Holy Spirit bring about change in our lives and most people do not like change. They are comfortable just as they are and do not want to take the risk associated with change.

Jesus came to announce to us that an identity based on success, popularity, and power is a false identity—an illusion! Loudly and clearly, He says, "You are not what the world makes you; but you are children of God." The spiritual life requires a constant claiming of our true identities. Our true identities are the beloved sons and daughters of our Heavenly Father.

Sad to say, the church has many scoffers today. The Catholic faith is ridiculed in speech, on talk shows, on television comedies, and in motion pictures. In the early days of the church, the scoffers persecuted and martyred believing Christians. Today, they just make fun. In the early days of the church, the believers came together to offer mass in homes, caves, and catacombs—wherever they could do so unnoticed by hostile eyes. Today, many Christians join in the laughter of those who ridicule the church. They stay home watching and enjoying those who make fun of our faith and rarely come to worship on Sundays and holy days.

Finally, there were those who responded to the apostles' testimony and the grace of the Holy Spirit. These are the ones who committed themselves to an active life of faith. They were the martyrs, the confessors, doctors, and saints whose lives continue to inspire us. Today, you who are present at mass stand on their shoulders and continue to do as they did: build up Christ's church by your living witness. At the feast of Pentecost, our Lord asks us to examine our consciences daily to make sure we are never numbered among the spectators or the scoffers.

The sacraments of initiation should make us proud to be Roman Catholics. Most problems in life can be traced back to poor self-image (identity). At the beginning of creation, God made us in His image and His likeness and proclaimed us very good. This is the first revealed truth and the rest of the Bible—God's passionate attempt to convince us of this truth. If we are authentically rooted in this identity as a child of God, we are well on our way to establishing a healthy life of intimacy and integrity.

Personal Identity

1. I am my authorities
2. I am my needs
3. I am my relationships
4. I am my self
5. I am public, private, and secret
6. I am a bundle of irrational thoughts and conflicting emotions
7. I am a touched sinner
8. I am made in the image and likeness of God

The Identity of Jesus

1. Jesus is Lord and Savior
2. Jesus is King
3. Jesus is Suffering Servant
4. Jesus is the Good Shepherd
5. Jesus is the Lamb of God
6. Jesus is fire
7. Jesus is living water
8. Jesus is Rabbi
9. Jesus is the gate, the alpha and omega, the way, the truth, the life
10. Jesus is the bread of life

20
INTIMACY

The Blessed Trinity is the mystery of mysteries before which even the seraphim veil their faces, singing with astonished wonder—"Holy, Holy, Holy." The universal church celebrates one of her central feasts on Trinity Sunday. It is the feast of the Most Holy Trinity. In honor of the Trinity, I begin my homilies in the name of the Father, and of the Son, and of the Holy Spirit.

What really matters is not the quality of our explanations, but the depth of our faith. The Blessed Trinity is a mystery—three persons, yet one God. No pope, no saint, no doctor of the church can understand this mystery.

There is a story about Saint Augustine walking along the shore in North Africa pondering how God could be one yet three. He comes upon a boy carrying a bucket of water to a small hole he had dug in the sand.

"Augustine watched him for a while and finally asked the child what he was doing. The child answered that he would scoop all the water from the sea and pour it into the little hole in the sand. 'What?' Augustine said. 'That is impossible. Obviously, the sea is too large and the hole too small.' 'Indeed,' said the child, 'but I will sooner draw all the water from the sea and empty it into this hole than you will succeed in penetrating the mystery of the Holy Trinity with your limited understanding.' Augustine turned away in amazement and when he looked back the child had disappeared."[46]

Let us pray that the Trinity will stir us to bow in reverence before all mystery, human, and divine.

In more than forty years of serving as a priest, I have observed most people I've met seek to live their lives more fully but are unsure how to satisfy this desire. They seek to live more meaningful lives in relationship with Father, Son, and Holy Spirit as well as with spouse, children, relatives, neighbors, religious community members, and/or the less fortunate, but do not know how. They do not know how to overcome inevitable obstacles that occur and recur: bitterness, jealousy, anger buried alive, fear, uncertainty, lack of confidence, loneliness, destructive patterns of living—abuse of alcohol, drugs, sexual addiction.

What can be done? Do I pray differently than when I first learned how to pray as a child? Am I like the seventy-year-old man or woman who accomplished much in his or her life but still has nagging questions: "Why do I feel empty? What help do I need to actively seek to grow spiritually? When do I have the time and energy to pray? Where concretely is there healthy love in my life—human and divine?"

Some people get the feeling that they are going to die without really loving. Below the surface they yearn for more peace, more joy, more forgiveness, more hope, and more love.

I've seen couples who got married and they were for all indications in love, but two years later, they couldn't stand each other. They get divorced without even trying to patch things up. That's the risk of intimacy. We can hurt our spouses more than anyone else in the world. That's the dark side of the joy of an intimate bond of love, of sharing closeness.

A married couple may feel they have drifted apart over

the years. They love each other—what choice do they have? But why is their love distant? They don't really communicate other than an exchange of information and that basic level even gets thwarted at times. There is no holy communion in that relationship.

How do couples grow old together and continue to deepen their love for each other? Does their marriage mask a life of alienation? Instead of embracing life, couples opt to run and hide from their true selves and one another. Why do we make activities other than love as our ultimate concern—sports, movies, music, cars, money. Why do so many people repress, minimize, or deny a life directed by the Holy Spirit? Why do we keep asking the same questions over and over again? There must be more to life than this.

Are you sharing common experiences? Are you also sharing common understanding of those experiences? What about common judgments? Are those judgments reasonable?

Be vigilant against what happens to many married couples called *circular reinforcement*. "I'll pretend that you (wife) are happy and secure if you pretend that I (husband) am happy and secure, and we will both pretend we are not pretending." This unspoken contract hides basic unhappiness and insecurity in a subtle, shallow, delusional way.

It's not a cookie cutter culture. People have to be deeply in touch with their values and ask themselves what they are willing to sacrifice in order to continue in a healthy, wholesome, humanizing relationship with spouse and children.

Why is pursuing the spiritual life so difficult? The spiritual life and spiritual maturity include such experiences as prayer, meditation, contemplation, worship, celebration, leisure, compassion, rest, faith, hope, and, above all, love. These are all key ingredients in the recipe for intimacy—with our spouses, with the Holy Spirit, with ourselves, with our neighbors.

But any list of ingredients can be thrown together any

which way and not turn out the way the recipe intended. That's why recipes have instructions. Your instructions for intimacy come from the example of our Blessed Mother. She welcomes each day with enthusiasm, laughter, wonder, and boundless love for everyone she meets. I am completely taken by her spirit of spontaneous joy.

Still, this recipe for intimacy can be enhanced through adoration, and the mode of adoration in this case is prayer; its culmination—the Eucharist. "No prayer is so difficult as the adoration of the Eucharist," said Carlo Carretto in his *Letters from the Desert*. "One's whole natural strength rebels against it ... the Eucharist is the silence of God, the weakness of God – to reduce Himself to Bread while the world is so noisy, so agitated, so confused."[47]

Jesus holds us accountable when we keep Him close to our hearts. Partaking in the ritual of the Eucharist is a good habit we can form in order to do so.

21

INTEGRITY

The light turned yellow, just in front of her. She did the right thing, stopping at the crosswalk, even though she could have beaten the red light by accelerating through the intersection. The tailgating man was furious and honked his horn, screaming in frustration, as he missed his chance to get through the intersection, dropping his cellphone and almost his cigarette.

As he was still mid-rant, he heard a tap on his window and looked up into the face of a very serious police officer. The officer ordered him to exit his car with his hands up. He took him to the police station where he was searched, fingerprinted, photographed, and placed in a holding cell.

After a few of hours, the man was escorted back to the booking desk where the arresting officer was waiting.

He said, "I'm very sorry for this mistake. You see, I pulled up behind your car while you were blowing your horn, gesturing to the woman in front of you, and cussing a blue streak. I noticed your 'What Would Jesus Do' and 'Follow Me to Sunday School' bumper stickers, the 'Choose Life' license plate holder, and the chrome-plated Christian fish emblem on the trunk, so naturally I assumed you had stolen the car."

"Morality like art," said G. K. Chesterton, "consists of drawing a line somewhere." We live in an age in which no lines seem to be drawn at all. If we take our sinning seriously, we may at least find that we can be interesting again.

Russian writer and historian Aleksandr I. Solzhenitsyn hypothesized that "the line separating good and evil passes not through states, nor between classes, nor between political parties either—but right through every human heart—and through all human hearts. This line shifts. Inside us, it oscillates with the years. And even within hearts overwhelmed by evil, one small bridgehead of good is retained. And even in the best of all hearts, there remains ... an un-uprooted small corner of evil."

Solzhenitsyn continues, "I have come to understand the truth of all the religions of the world: They struggle with the evil inside a human being (inside every human being). It is impossible to expel evil from the world in its entirety, but it is possible to constrict it within each person."[48]

When will we finally overcome racism and division? I believe that when we deal with one another in love, we are not only acting in an ethically upright manner, but we are moving in sync with the deepest rhythms of creation. Hence, there is no such thing as "your" problem.

If there is one person who dies through violence, we are all violated. When will we all learn and practice this basic truth?

We have specific examples of Jesus, Gandhi, and Martin Luther King, Jr. speaking peace and nonviolence to those who had betrayed and killed them. These three figures offer us a legitimate option: bring order and unity—not through violence—through human compassion and generous love. Forgiveness, truth telling, and works of mercy are all modes of a nonviolent lifestyle available to everyone.

When we align our minds, words, and bodies to the nonviolent energy of creation, a new world is established.

22

LEISURE

"Accept from the holy people of God the gifts to be offered to Him. Know what you are doing, and imitate the mystery you celebrate: model your life on the mystery of the Lord's cross."
—*Priesthood Ordination Rite: presentation of paten and chalice*

In Sacred Scripture, "to remember" is a holy act. It means to make events or happenings from the past come alive now. What events or happenings? All that Jesus did by way of example for us: helping the poor, healing the sick, forgiving the sinner, reaching out to the outcast ... Whenever we come together as a Christian for the Eucharist, our faith tells us, assures us, that what we share is the body and blood of Jesus Himself. We also share who we are for one another—that we are to be sustenance and support for one another.

We do not become a Christian community by sliding into a pew. Rather, we become a Christian community by welcoming others, by reaching out beyond ourselves to stand in solidarity with the poor and the outcast, and by encouraging the diversity within our community.

There are many kinds of hungers: physical, emotional, and

spiritual. Let us commit ourselves to take time to reflect first on how Jesus has satisfied our hungers by giving us His body and blood as food for our journey to Heaven. Let us also commit ourselves to satisfy the hungers of those around us by responding the first time someone calls, by praying for a friend and for an enemy, by writing the letter we so long avoided, by volunteering our time at school, a hospital, a soup kitchen, by mentoring a child, by meeting a person we have ignored.

Yes, let's work at it and discover new ways to feed others in our community. Only then will we be acting as Eucharistic people joined in a covenant sealed by the blood of Christ. By doing this, we make Christ's body and blood a most intimate part of ourselves. We become one with Christ and we become one with each other, truly the body and blood of Christ, Corpus Christi.

Walking the path of Jesus Christ is a time commitment and a balance. Because we are called to serve a higher good and help our neighbors in need, we are also called to have life and live it abundantly. One cannot succeed or proceed without the other. Leisure and rest are important to keep the mind sharp and to help discern in the most clear and intentional way.

American Catholic Benedictine monk, author, and lecturer David Steindl-Rast says in his *Essential Writings*, "If there is no leisure, there is no love. Leisure is not the privilege of those who have time, but the *virtue* of those who take time. Leisure is a fundamental restfulness about who we are, where we are and what we do."[49]

We must work leisurely. We must drive a car leisurely and not act like we're always in a race to beat everybody else on the road. We must cook a meal leisurely. Leisure allows us to savor the moment.

I admire people who rarely get frazzled. Most people put self-induced pressure on themselves to perform in the best way, in the quickest way, and in the most efficient way. The opposite of leisure is efficiency. You have an appointment and you're just coming from a meeting. A leisurely person knows how to shift gears from one activity to the next while still giving his or her undivided attention.

When Jesus was on his three-year-long mission, he could engage demons, crowds, His inner circle, and then He could engage people who were out to get Him. Even His neighbors in Nazareth wanted to run him out of town, let alone the sect of the pharisees, the sect of the Herodians, the Sadducees. They got angry. Who does he think He is? Yet, nothing could shake Him. Instead, He accepted the challenge. Nothing anyone could say or do was going to prevent Him from doing this healing work and not be compromised by a mob mentality and crowds.

A leisurely person has a remarkable level of flexibility, because he or she is not putting excessive pressure on his or herself. For many years of my life, I was hyper-competitive. I put that pressure on myself because I had it in my mind that I wanted to honor my father, who couldn't play sports because of his poor health.

A spiritually immature person is busy. That busyness is not busy with one singular activity. No, this is a frenetic type of busyness, a compulsive type of busyness. It is trying to prove to everyone how busy you are. It is the need to feel needed. Leisure is being at peace with the time we have, the gifts we've been granted, and the love around us which makes us whole.

VI
ORDINARY TIME

John's Gospel is filled with beginnings and endings.

"In the beginning was the Word" (John 1:1)

"It is finished" (John 19:30)

But, of course, our Lord's work wasn't finished. The resurrection marked a new beginning; newness was evident everywhere; joy was contagious as now everyone had the experience of seeing the Risen Lord.

Even the final chapters of this Gospel are about endings and beginnings.

Chapter 20 seems to be a fitting ending.

"Now Jesus did many other signs in the presence of [his] disciples that are not written in this book. But these are written that you may [come to] believe that Jesus is the Messiah, the Son of God, and that through this belief you may have life in his name." (John 20:30-31).

We're ready to close the book, but there's one more chapter.

It seems to me that the conclusion in chapter 20 brings to a close all Jesus did in the presence of His disciples during the public ministry after the resurrection.

Chapter 21 is not a conclusion at all, though it looks like one. Actually, chapter 21 is the beginning of the ongoing story of all the many other things Jesus continues to do and which could never be recounted adequately even if a whole world of books were to be written. Chapter 21 is about what is still going on:

- The unfaltering obedience required of all disciples to Jesus's word
- The perpetual fruitfulness in ministry that will bring salvation to the whole world Jesus was sent to save
- The uninterrupted sharing in the life of Jesus through the contemplative experience of the Eucharist

Jesus comes to us in this dramatic scene on Lake Tiberius. In the ordinary, burdensome work of His disciples, He manifests Himself in a simple meal—making of it a sublime moment of contemplation that those who participated in it would never forget.

Jesus's whole life was a movement back and forth between the contemplative and the active;

doing the will of the Father each day meant that He had to take time apart, in a space apart—even if it meant rising very early in the morning.

Doing the will of the Father brought loud cries and tears. What specifically brought the loud cries and tears? Sickness, disease, slavery, and evil, but not in the abstract:

- Simon's mother-in-law
- Leper who dared defy all convention
- Possessed boy and grieving father
- Young girl thought to be dead
- Woman with internal bleeding
- Centurion pleading for his servant
- People under cruel yoke to tyranny
- Evil men like Antipas, Caiaphas, Pilate
- The despised prostitute who washed Jesus' feet in the house of a Pharisee
- The traitorous tax collectors (Mathew and Zaccheus)
- Lazarus' death- brother of Martha and Mary
- Calvary

Yes, He is our high priest who can sympathize with our weaknesses, and every one of these acts of mercy and dealing in His public ministry was also a moment pregnant with contemplative meaning and fruitfulness.

Everyone Jesus met, the good and the evil, felt special in His presence. No matter how sick, weary, or guilt-ridden a person felt, Jesus held out the promise of new life.

He touched them all and summoned their hidden talents back to life. He invited them to see the great possibilities in themselves. He gave them a sense of their extraordinary dignity. They became brothers and sisters to Him—people he called by name. He took their brokenness, their frailty, their weakness, and their sins and raised them up to new life. They could never settle for a mediocre, ordinary life again. He helped them experience the newness and exhilaration of resurrection life.

Being immersed in the Risen Lord means being immersed in goodness, truth, beauty, unity, and love. These five virtues do not come cheap. In fact, to sustain these five virtues in one's life will prove quite costly. However, the cost will be like discovering the "fine pearl" and the "hidden treasure" in the field. You will be able to discern and resist evil. You will become one with Jesus and learn to recognize Him in the suffering, in the poor, in the "little ones" of this world.

Our ability to receive the church's teaching in the proper spirit of discipleship, that is, being a committed lifelong student of Jesus, the Master Teacher, will enable us to "seek first the Kingdom of God."

We need to remain faithful to the today of the church, not the yesterday or the tomorrow. "This is the day the Lord has made, let us rejoice and be glad," instructs the Psalmist.

Ordinary time in the liturgical life of the church, and in the reading of the New Testament is rarely ordinary. Grace overflows on our daily human condition and uplifts us in everyday life experiences.

23
ATTENTIVE

An elderly man in his eighties hurried to his doctor appointment at 8 a.m. He wanted to finish quickly because he had to be somewhere by 9. Dr. Tobin asked Bob about his next appointment. Bob proudly said that at 9 a.m. every morning, he visits the nursing home to eat breakfast with his wife, Ann. The doctor asked about his wife's condition. Bob said that his wife had Alzheimer's disease, and for the past five years she hasn't known who he was. Dr. Tobin was surprised and asked Bob why he continues to go faithfully if she has no idea who he is. Bob replied, "Because I still know who she is!"

No one in the world has escaped the COVID-19 pandemic of 2020 without having their lives significantly changed. Across the United States, there has been profound sadness and fear, whether for a lost loved one or a loss of the way things were.

As we began to restart life after months of stay-at-home orders, I reminded my community that we should not forget to mourn. I believe we need to set aside a time to grieve nationally, locally, or both. That requires a meaningful, mindful ritual.

How and when to implement these rituals is unclear. It is difficult to begin the process of grieving when the end seems to change daily. Even beyond the time of the publication of this book, are we still a long way from being able to gather "en masse" in public spaces to hold a peaceful, candlelight vigil?

Mourning is a time when community is most needed, because video conferences and live-streams too often remind us of our isolation instead of creating real connectedness. When it is finally safe, we need to gather the bodies in churches, stadiums, and concert halls. And whether the presider is a priest, politician, or point guard, we need public prayers and moments of community silence to mourn and honor everything and everyone who has been lost.

Once mourning has run its course, it is essential for our attentiveness to shift from faith, memory, and love to gratitude.

Thanksgiving is always the fourth Thursday in November, but giving thanks knows no time or season. It is not a phrase, but a frame of reference. It is not a pious sentiment, but a realistic outlook on life. Thanksgiving is a rich, traditional celebration for our country and our faith. The Eucharistic meal and the Thanksgiving meal we celebrate with our families speak the same language and offer us a nourishing and sustaining result.

The first Thanksgiving Day meal celebrated by the Pilgrims and the Native Americans reminds us clearly that:

- Hardships and obstacles can be overcome
- Differences can be resolved peacefully
- People of diverse cultures, languages, and ways of thinking can share together in a generous manner

In the Eucharistic meal, Jesus shared with His disciples.

In summary, He said, "I am sharing my life and love with you, totally and completely. If you do this in memory of Me in your own lives, you, too, will overcome any obstacle and difficult crises that might occur. You, too, will believe that you count, you matter, you can make a difference. You, too, will experience peace, trust, hope and liberation."

When Jesus set about to proclaim the kingdom, His pulpit was often a supper table. Dozens of passages are found in the Gospels referring to Jesus's meals, food, or to eating. Somewhat surprisingly, perhaps, most of these meals were controversial. The good people didn't like those with whom Jesus was eating, or what He was doing at those meals. In fact, a good deal of the opposition that Jesus stirred up came because of His ministry of meal fellowship, a most characteristic element of His public ministry.

The Eucharist is such a central part of our tradition and our faith life that it has ceased to startle, ceased to challenge, ceased to pain. It has become a very comfortable and easy part of our lives. We forget that even at the miraculous feeding of the multitude, Jesus insisted that the disciples give food to the people to eat. He also told us at the Last Supper that we should continue to do in His memory what He had done for us—a gift that implies pain and suffering.

Unless the Eucharist flows from daily life and enriches the same, it is meaningless for people. Unless it has something to say about extending Christ's love and compassion to a needy world, it becomes a private party. Unless it opens us to be nailed to the cross of our own pride and selfishness, Christ's blood will have been shed in vain. Unless it compels us to build a new and better world, it is just an empty ritual.

Jesus challenges us to be attentive to all of these things. The Holy Spirit guides us to smile inward, smile outward, relax our bodies, and be alert (attentive) in our thinking.

If we do not remain attentive in our thinking, we succumb

to the seduction of the Evil Spirit. We open ourselves up to stress, which triggers a great feeling of oppression, although Jesus came for us to have life and have it in abundance. The sad thing is that oppression's default setting is to seek escape and we often encounter darkness in that pursuit, because projection is the desperate alternative we frequently find.

24
INTELLIGENT

May my teaching soak in like the rain, and my utterance drench like the dew, Like a downpour upon the grass, like a shower upon the crops.
　–Deuteronomy 32:2

Stories connect us to our souls. They are healing to our spirits, enriching to our imaginations. Parables are like jokes: they have one point, and you either get it or you don't. The difference is, a parable calls for an immediate yet calculated decision.

I am reminded of the story of the mother and father taking a trip with their six-year-old son. It was a hot summer day. The traffic was heavy and there were long periods of waiting. The boy became completely fragmented; a burden to himself and an irritation to his parents. He desperately needed a story. When they reached their destination, the mother, realizing her son's need, told him the story of Hansel and Gretel. The boy listened wide-eyed and silent. Afterward, calmly he went out to play. He had lost touch with his soul on the tedious ride. The story brought him back to center.

Years ago, I met a man named Vincent. he was homeless.

FATHER TOM HERON

He had no real address. However, he did have a sense of community. Vincent was one among the many homeless people who lived on the Philadelphia side of the Ben Franklin Bridge. He lived in a Kenmore refrigerator box marked with the words "Fragile, Handle with Care." Vincent claimed those words as his address. He reminded me that those words were everyone's address.

Vincent would say, over and over, that when we see all people as fragile, then we will know how to treat people. When we see ourselves as fragile, we will see ourselves in all people. Vincent, without a home, really believed that this view of ourselves and one another is the way of love.

He had no health care, but he knew how to heal humanity's wounds. He did not have enough good food to eat, but he could nourish anyone he met. His sight was limited, but his vision of the world was bright and clear. What a remarkable man living in a refrigerator box—a tabernacle of sorts—a living and visible real presence of the word made flesh—broken, shared, and poured out in love and simplicity.

This was a man wise beyond his years. He exhibited purity through his intelligence. Yet, we nonchalantly, numbly bucket homeless people in the "unintelligent" category each and every day. Unconscious bias is spiritual immaturity at its core. Intelligence gives us a chance to see all of the points of views. Intelligence allows us to give our brothers and sisters the benefit of the doubt rather than a harsh judgment from the onset based on appearance or social status.

Intelligence is perception. The evangelists—Matthew, Mark, Luke, and John—are the cornerstone of intelligence in biblical teaching. An outline of their wisdom of the life of Jesus of Nazareth shows just that:

Jesus was born in Bethlehem, grew up in Nazareth, called disciples at the Sea of Galilee, worshipped in synagogues throughout the region, ate meals with friends Mary, Martha, and Lazarus in Bethany, attended a wedding at Cana, told parables in Jericho, prayed in Gethsemane and many "out of the way places," led a procession down the Mount of Olives, taught in the Jerusalem temple, was violently crucified on a hill called Golgatha, and three days later, broke bread with Cleopas and his companion in Emmaus.

Because of these facts, we are not free to make up our own private spiritualities. We know too much about Jesus's life and spirituality. The story of Jesus gives us several ordinary incidents and simple words, specific with places, times, and names—all of them interwoven to reveal human/divine truth. Jesus prevents us from thinking that life is a matter of ideas to ponder and concepts to discuss. Jesus encourages us to use the spiritual intelligence we have to trust the intuition of the Holy Spirit so that we may make the right decisions for ourselves and in consideration of others all the days of our lives.

Gospel Paradoxes

DIE TO LIVE

BE LAST IN ORDER TO BE FIRST

BE EMPTY IN ORDER TO BE FULL

BE POOR IN ORDER TO BE RICH

BE WEAK IN ORDER TO BE STRONG

BE FOOLISH IN ORDER TO BE WISE

25

REASONABLE

A wise person knows to put things into perspective (intelligence), but a still wiser person knows what perspective to put them into (being reasonable). For example, a doctor who tells the widow of a patient who has just died that, "After all, your husband's death was only one of 2.8 million deaths this year in the United States," is in need of bedside sensitivity. On the other hand, an epidemiologist who tries to express his deep compassion for every death that he encounters will never progress beyond his first statistical table. The proper perspective changes with context.

Most people navigate between complacency and panic. Follow the medical/scientific data in order to reach a fully rational viewpoint. But, of course, neither science nor the world is like this. How do we form a moving viewpoint that gives us a healthy, livable perspective?

Medical science is often an inexact science that at its worst perspective can be used as a powerful tool for the bullying of a population that does not have the time, interest, or talent to dive deep into the moving analytics. How do we match a common sense realm of meaning with a theoretical sense realm of meaning? Bernard Lonergan would say: be attentive to your experience, be intelligent to your understanding, be **reasonable** in the judgments you make, in order to make sound decisions.

Spirituality is as real as science. For some, science is the key to a full life. For others, spirituality is the focus for living life abundantly.

We live in a world where what is real has been reduced to what is physical, to what can be measured, seen, touched, tasted, and smelled. As a result, many people can become spiritually tone-deaf, where all the goods are reduced to a flat screen.

Prayer is a struggle and so are a lot of other activities. When the flat screen is our leading source of enjoyment, it is difficult to be attracted to anything, to see depth, to be deeply touched by mystery, poetry, faith, and love.

How does Father, Son, and Holy Spirit become as real as the flat screen? How do we connect with our souls every day? How do we discover deep meaning in our daily relationships with one another?

How do we get beyond living, a drab, dutiful life, replaying heartaches and headaches over and over again?

The spiritually mature approach is to be compassionate and brutally honest with facts and to be courageous, humble, and united in making decisions that positively impact both the individual and the common good.

26

RESPONSIBLE

I am reminded of the story of the father who one morning knocks on his son's bedroom door and says, "Jamie, wake up!"

Jamie answers, "I don't want to get up."

The father impatiently shouts, "Get up, you have to go to school."

"I don't want to go to school."

"Why not?"

"Three reasons," says Jamie. "First, because it's so dull; second, because the kids tease me; and third, I hate it."

"Well, I am going to give you three reasons why you **must** go to school. First, because it is your duty; second because you are forty-five years old, and third, because you're the principal."

Our Heavenly Father gives the Holy Spirit to each of us because He is, in essence, self-donation. It is the nature of God, Father, Son and Holy Spirit, to give.

As human beings whose human spirits are joined to the Holy Spirit, we are encouraged to cooperate generously with this unmerited goodness of God. A spiritually mature person has learned the art and science of responding to the impulse of the Holy Spirit. What might the impulse of the Spirit look like?

1. Suggesting that we be pleasant and welcoming rather than ornery—when ornery is how we're feeling
2. To be generous in a given situation rather than miserly or cheap

As we begin to grow in an awareness of the Holy Spirit in our daily lives, a charism—a gift of God's grace—is given us. Gradually and quietly we observe ourselves more attentive to our thoughts, our feelings and our will. We begin being able to recognize (discern) a thought as coming from the Ego Spirit, the Evil Spirit, or the Holy Spirit.

A spiritually mature person also recognizes the need to develop and nurture a daily prayer-life. That discipline, achieved through effort and blessed by the grace of the Holy Spirit, will serve us our whole life long.

We will become comfortable with silence and solitude, which allows the Holy Spirit access to our innermost beings and while the tension between good and evil will persist, these tiny impulses of the Holy Spirit will take effect in our lives. Imperceptivity at first, our acting on the influence of the Holy Spirit will help us die to the Ego, to relegate it to a lesser place in our Christian life.

St. Paul uses *kenosis*—a technical word—especially in the third chapter of his letter to the Philippians, which means to empty oneself out of the ego and wrongheaded tendencies so that one can create space for *plemora*—the fullness of the love of Father, Son, and Holy Spirit. That enables us to become what we are all called to become: a contemporary Christ man/a contemporary Christ woman.

I recently found myself driving in a notoriously bad neighborhood in West Philadelphia. As I was stopped at a red light, I observed a pleasant man approaching each car asking for money so he could eat. He told me he was very hungry. I had two pieces of nutritious fig bars. I rolled down the window and gave them to him, but from my observation, it appeared he regretted he said he was very hungry at all.

I found myself at a common crossroads: I could have not acknowledged he was there, decided not to roll down the window, or refused to give him anything.

A responsible, spiritually mature person still looks a person in the eye, even if he or she is a stranger. Even if I could not make a responsible judgment on whether he was honestly hungry or that was his gig, I had to make a decision to follow the impulse of the Holy Spirit. The nudge I was given by the Holy Spirit was to be humane.

Spiritually immature individuals place blame. They have embraced, full tilt, the victim card and the victim mentality. An immature person never takes responsibility for his or her thoughts, feelings, words, or actions.

A mature Christian knows how to navigate the weeds and wheat of his or her life. We all have an Achilles heel, a weak spot. For some, it may be a fixation on money or a fear of lack. That so drives an individual; however, Jesus admonishes us to seek first the Kingdom of God (Matthew 6:33) and all the rest will fall into place.

Each day living into spiritual maturity requires an examination of conscience—the practice of seeing and analyzing the varied motivations that determine our choices. Docile to the work of the Holy Spirit, our patterns of thoughts, speech, and behavior will become ordered. No longer will they control us.

None of us has merited the gift of the Holy Spirit. With an increased awareness of what has been bestowed on us comes a clearer consciousness of when and how the Spirit acts in our lives. And from this rises a greater responsibility for us to fulfill what has been impressed on our hearts.

The gratuitous gifts of the Spirit have been given to us freely by virtue of Jesus's suffering, death, resurrection, and ascension. Once we are conscious of these great gifts, we are able to give what's been given! With a growing awareness of what the Holy Spirit is asking of us comes a greater responsibility to make response.

In necessariis unitas, in dubiis libertas, in omnibus caritas.

"Unity in necessary things; freedom in doubtful things; love in all things."

27

MYSTICISM

Mysticism is wisdom found through love. It is the simple intuition of the truth. Mysticism is a way of life in which a person faces his or her own inner emptiness, destroys the illusion of self-worship, and reorients his or her entire life to God, others, and the world.

There is a story about a young man named Jim who was in search of God. Because of so much confusion in his life, Jim didn't know where to turn. He heard of a hermit who lived at an isolated desolate beach. Jim went to visit the hermit and asked if he could be his disciple.

The hermit led him to the ocean, plunged him into the water, and held his head under the water for a considerable amount of time. The young man tried to gain his composure after he was finally released.

The hermit asked him what he wanted most of all while he was under the water. "Air," he said. "Yes," said the hermit. "Return home and come back to me when you desire God as much as you desired air just now."

There is something somber and sober about the month of November. In the world of nature, autumn pushes relentlessly toward winter. The chilly winds tell us that snow and ice are on the way.

In our liturgical world, November is identified in the minds of many as the month of the Holy Souls. We pray for the faithful departed with the firm hope that God will hear our prayers and grant them eternal rest. We celebrate the feasts of All Saints and All Souls, which draw us into one of the most consoling doctrines of the Roman Catholic faith, the Communion of Saints.

The approach of winter and the memory of departed parents, relatives, and friends can cast a pall over our lives. Nature and liturgy combine to direct our thoughts to a thirty-day meditation on death. Death has many dark sides to it. At the death of someone we love, we struggle with sorrow and grief. Despite the reassurances that faith gives and that Jesus gave to His apostles, death is an awesome, frightening event. Death brings us directly into an unavoidable confrontation with the mysteriousness of life.

Yet, as St. Ambrose states, "We should have a daily familiarity with death, a daily desire for death." Death can lift our eyes to eternity. It teaches us that nothing in this world lasts forever except the love of the Blessed Trinity. Death is the final breakthrough in the passionate pilgrimage toward the kingdom of heaven. Life will continue to escape us until we face death and embrace its terror.

If you have faith and the sacraments, you are rich with a wealth that does not perish. Embracing death leads you deeper into the mystery of life—the ultimate paradox of the Christian way of living.

On All Souls' Day we recall and act on the truth that our prayers help those deceased who still move through purification toward the fullness of life. This feast reminds us that charity goes beyond the boundaries of this world. Every time we celebrate the Eucharist, we do more than remember the dead, our loved ones, and the saints. We unite with them in a spiritual, mystical union. The paschal mystery pervades everything we do. It is inversely proportional.

So, now we find ourselves in November and the end time: the end of growth in nature, our own end in death, the end of the church year, and the end of time. We face these endings with joy and hope because of our trust in the paschal mystery of our Lord Jesus Christ.

The relationship between asceticism and mysticism is a practice or way of life that involves a systematic self-denial for some ideal. We must renounce the comforts of society and lead a life of discipline. Asceticism is a self-willed, rigorous, pious, devotional practice that becomes reactionary and projected onto others. Mysticism is achieved by following the impulses of the Holy Spirit.

Are you willing to forsake the world in favor of salvation and eternal life?

AFTERWORD

According to a citation by Fr. Bernard Lonergan, S.J. of the Louvain psychologist, Albert Vergote, "a person reaches genuine religious faith about the age of thirty."[51] In my experience and judgment, many people do not truly reach religious, moral, and intellectual maturity until around forty. I would hold that same timeline for spiritual maturity, especially if a person is making a conscious effort to grow spiritually.

We are here because we share in the dream of Jesus of Nazareth and by our participation in the liturgy, we acknowledge that we will not allow this dream to atrophy.

We are all engaged in a program of helping Jesus realize His dream. The Blessed Trinity might be invisible to us at times, but with the eyes of a child, with the constancy of a mature believer, we pledge ourselves to remain faithful to this dream as Jesus Himself did, realizing that perhaps the maddest thing of all is to see life as it is and not as it should be—a paradox at its core.

Paradox involves creative tension, bringing together two assertions, which appear to conflict. The Gospel teaches us that these ironic ideas are how we grow in spiritual maturity:

AFTERWORD

- In order to be strong, we must be weak
- In order to be first, we must be last
- In order to live, we must die to ourselves
- In order to be rich, we must be willing to be poor
- In order to be fruitful, we must be barren
- We must fight against hate with love
- We must be willing to feel foolish in order to become wiser
- In order to be full, we must empty our souls
- In order to have the most personal experience, we must think universally
- And most crucial: anything we may consider a burden is a gift—a blessing—from the Holy Spirit

It is usually difficult to trace the complex interests and actions of one's adult life to specific experience in childhood and youth. Yet, for me, I cannot help but link my interest in divine love, in faith, in sports, in how and why people behave the way they do, in the unpredictability of motivation, and the persistence of memory—to the death of my dad, who was just thirty-three years old when he was born into eternal life.

We all regress back to spiritual immaturity from time to time. How do we break through to spiritual maturity and how do we sustain it? Like prayer, there's no universal blueprint.

Mercy is a major obstacle that Jesus handled very well. It has to be part of our lives, yet it's a major stumbling block. We cannot forgive a parent, a boss, a teacher, or even ourselves. However, not being able to forgive yourself is the worst, because you wallow in guilt and shame.

Once the light goes on that our Lord has forgiven us, who are we not to forgive people who have wronged us? All of our sins, all tied up and bundled into one, are still woefully deficient in comparison to God's ability to show grace and forgiveness.

When we can let go, we empty our souls to make room

for faith, hope, and love. They are theological virtues. They are God-given gifts. You can't go out and manufacture faith. You can only grow in faith, in hope, and in love to the degree that you're growing in your relationship with Father, Son, and Holy Spirit.

There are four signposts in the spiritual life:

The call – It begins with a call that never ends! For some it is clearly marked, for others not so distinct, but for all a gradual awakening to a sense of incompleteness:

- an awareness of an absence
- a sense of something vacant and unfulfilled
- a strange restlessness
- an unarticulated longing for something that seems both unattainable yet just within grasp

More people hear this call than answer it. In our society all too many assume that this feeling of incompleteness is a call for a material or physical need and that same society invites them to fill that vacuum with drink, drugs, sexual encounters, food, fast cars, etc. None of which works. You know that and so do they, often when it is too late.

Be prepared to answer *the call* each day. Mary is our model here. She was always ready whenever the Holy Spirit called her deeper and deeper into the mystery of her vocation.

The second signpost: *The Holy Spirit is at work long before we know it; long before we do anything. We often think we are the ones in search of the Blessed Trinity.*

Living on the edge brings an awareness that all along we were not the hunter but the hunted. A transforming moment.

To remember this is to stop trying to get the Blessed Trinity to do something we think needs to be done. Now we can let God be the hunter while we become more aware of what the Blessed Trinity is trying to do so that we can respond to it and participate and take delight in it.

AFTERWORD

But there is a catch with this signpost. When the Holy Spirit is shaping and molding, it will be sometimes painful. However, it is Divinely-willed, Divinely-directed. Again, Mary is the model. She was told about a sword that would pierce her heart. Still, she said, **FIAT.** She saw in her own vocation—the vocation of her Son—and she was faithful to the end.

Be faithful to your call. It's an everyday event and will always catch you off guard—when you are about your ordinary duties as the first disciples were—fishing, mending nets, collecting taxes. Be ready. Be attuned.

Remember Jesus calls you not for your strength, but for your surrender.

The third signpost is *not to be afraid of the Father's transforming love.*

Every person, who claims to be a disciple of the Lord—no exceptions—is called to be a holy person. Moses's call was the burning bush. Many would probably douse the bush and then, realizing their mistake, spend the rest of their lives trying to rekindle it.

Others feel called to approach as Moses did; feel pulled to the center. But fear takes over. We are afraid to move into the center because we see there an all-consuming fire. We do not want to lose ourselves in it.

Mary was afraid but still said yes. Hers was a faith that never wavered, a faith firm in the face of uncertainties, a love suffering faith all throughout her life.

One of the most difficult things is to allow ourselves to be loved. Mary allowed for the Father's transforming love to take over her life. Something momentous happened. Mary conceived in her womb Jesus, but also in her mind and in her heart an inner revelation took place. She accepted the call, her vocation, and her destiny. In that lies her greatness.

The fourth signpost is *living life on the edge, which means being still amidst all the surrounding chaos.*

AFTERWORD

Ever notice that within the Gospel accounts of Mary's encounters with Jesus there is little or no dialogue? Their relationship was such that they did not have to communicate with a lot of words. Theirs was a relationship we could characterize as silent stillness.

It was Jesus' enemies who did all the talking; who were engaged in ceaseless activity, clamorous agitation.

Mary in her stillness was always there supporting her Son with her quiet strength, following to the end the path he took in obedience to his Father's will. It was the activity of the mob that brought death; it was the stillness of Jesus and Mary that brought life.

Action without prayer is blind and dangerous. Prayer demands effort and energy. It challenges our laziness and superficiality, our reluctance to leave the realm of the transitory and live in the kingdom of Heaven.

In 1976, I started my second year of theological studies. Throughout the course of this academic year, my spiritual director, Fr. Dan Murray, gave me ten questions to ponder. He asked me to submit written responses to these questions as preparation for my ordination of Diaconate in May of 1977.

I began this book with a list of questions to ask of yourself. Now that you have learned and grown in spiritual maturity, I ask that you again ponder another set of questions—those same ten that Fr. Murray asked of me.

1. What does the word "death" mean to you?
2. What do you fear most about death?
3. How does death have power over you?
4. What does the word "Easter" mean to you?
5. How do you picture the resurrection of the body?
6. What will heaven be like?

AFTERWORD

7. What are you asked to believe when you profess "Jesus is not here, He is risen!"?
8. How do you participate in the crucified and risen life of Jesus?
9. List three reasons why you believe in the resurrection of Jesus
10. List three reasons why you or others do not believe in the resurrection

*"Let us, then, be children no longer, tossed here and there, carried about by every wind of doctrine that originates in human trickery and skill in proposing error. Rather, let us profess the truth in love and **grow to the full maturity of Christ** the head. Through him the whole body grows, and with the proper functioning of the members joined firmly together by each supporting ligament, builds itself up in love." (Ephesians 4: 14-16)[51]*

ACKNOWLEDGMENTS

I wish to acknowledge my gratitude to those who offered constructive criticism, especially Kevin Haslam, Mary Kay McKenna, Sara Lessard, Marie Baranowski, Val DiGiovanni, and Phil Ricci. Their input improved the quality of the book.

ABOUT THE AUTHOR

J. Thomas Heron is a Philadelphia Archdiocesan Priest. He has served in his current role as pastor of the newly formed St. Matthew Parish in Conshohocken, Pa., since 2014.

In 1978, Heron received a Master of Divinity degree, followed by a Master of Arts degree in religious studies in 1982 – both from St. Charles Seminary.

Following his ordination, Heron served in various assignments, including parochial vicar at St. Michael the Archangel (Levittown, 1978-82), teacher at Archbishop Kennedy High School (Conshohocken, 1982-86), school minister at Bishop McDevitt High School (Wyncote, 1986-89), Formation Faculty at St. Charles Borromeo Seminary (1989-96), parochial vicar at Saint Cyril (East Lansdowne, 1996-97), pastor at Good Shepherd Parish (Philadelphia, 1998-2003), pastor at St. Gabriel's (Norwood, 2003-07), parochial vicar at St. Pius X (Broomall, 2008-09), pastor at St. James (Elkins Park, 2009-10), parochial vicar at St. Coleman's (Ardmore, 2010-11), and parochial administrator at St. Matthew Church

(Conshohocken, 2011-12), and pastor at St. Matthew Church (Conshohocken, 2012-14), prior to the formation of the newly merged parish, which includes the former churches of Ss Cosmas and Damian, St. Gertrude, and St. Mary's.

An Introductory Guide to Spiritual Maturity is his second book.

ALSO BY FATHER TOM HERON

We Are All Called is the culmination of a series of life experiences for Father J. Thomas Heron, forty-plus years a priest. When Fr. Heron was just four years old, his dad died of heart failure. This significant life event forced Fr. Heron to mature at a young age, but also led him to ask many important questions. Had it not been for the vital spiritual and vocational mentors in his life, he may have never learned how to cope with tragedy and death—which he has now seen many times over—with grace and goodness. Fr. Heron believes in e.e. cummings' mantra, "we cannot be born enough"—that we all experience many births in life, and that we are all called by the Blessed Trinity to realize our places in salvation history, while carrying out our personal destinies. He is hopeful you will shed tears of joy and tears of empathy as you read his collection of stories, and ultimately realize many truths in your own life.

WORKS CITED

1. Kazantzakis, Nikos, and P. A. Bien. *Report to Greco*. London: Faber, 2001.
2. "Wrestling with God." Ron Rolheiser Wrestling with God Comments. Accessed November 30, 2020. http://ronrolheiser.com/wrestling-with-god/.
3. Team, Almaany. "Translation and Meaning of Αγιότητα in Almaany English-Greek Dictionary." almaany.com. Accessed November 30, 2020. https://www.almaany.com/en/dict/en-el/αγιότητα/.
4. Anonymous. "October: Confidence." Essay. In *A Year with the Saints*, 328. United States: P.J. Kenedy, 1891.
5. Guardini, Romano. *Meditations before Mass*, 91. Christian Classics Inc, 2014.
6. Rilke, Rainer Maria. *Letters to a Young Poet*, 21. United States: Dover Publications, 2012.
7. O'Connor, Flannery. *Mystery and manners; occasional prose*, 151. Japan: Farrar, Straus and Giroux, 1969.
8. *New American Standard Bible: New Testament*. Longview, TX: Word for the World, 1972.
9. Stone, Joshua David. *Soul Psychology: How to Clear Negative Emotions and Spiritualize Your Life*,

65. United Kingdom: Random House Publishing Group, 2010.
10. *New International Version*. Colorado Springs, Col.: International Bible Society, 1984.
11. Yutang, Lin. *My Country and My People*, 328. London: William Heineman Ltd., 1948.
12. Horn, Trent. "St. Ignatius Said What?," August 3, 2019. https://www.catholic.com/magazine/online-edition/st-ignatius-said-what.
13. Brown, Christopher M. "Thomas Aquinas (1224/6—1274)." Accessed November 30, 2020. https://www.iep.utm.edu/aquinas/.
14. *The Oxford Handbook of William Wordsworth*, 98. United Kingdom: Oxford University Press, 2015.
15. Wiederkehr, Macrina. *A Tree Full of Angels: Seeing the Holy in the Ordinary*, 111. United Kingdom: Harper & Row, 1988.
16. *The New American Bible*. New York: P.J. Kenedy & Sons, 1970.
17. Eliot, T.S. "Little Gidding." T. S. Eliot's "Little Gidding". Accessed November 30, 2020. http://www.columbia.edu/itc/history/winter/w3206/edit/tseliotlittlegidding.html.
18. Pinilis, Post author By Loren. "A Bibilical View of Time: Shifting from Chronos to Kairos." A Bibilical View of Time: Shifting from Chronos to Kairos - Life of a Steward. Accessed November 30, 2020. https://www.lifeofasteward.com/chronos-kairos/.
19. Popova, Maria. "James Baldwin's Advice on Writing." Brain Pickings, May 22, 2017. https://www.brainpickings.org/2016/02/08/james-baldwin-advice-on-writing/.
20. "Did George Carlin Pen 'The Paradox of Our Time'?" Snopes.com, August 10, 2020.

https://www.snopes.com/fact-check/the-paradox-of-our-time/.
21. Ibid.
22. Ibid.
23. Ibid.
24. Hemingway, Ernest. *A Farewell to Arms: The Hemingway Library Edition*, 318. United Kingdom: Scribner, 2012.
25. Greenberg, Sidney. *Say Yes to Life: A Book of Thoughts for Better Living*, 25. United States: Jason Aronson, Incorporated, 1999.
26. Bonhoeffer, Dietrich. "Readings: Letters and Papers from Prison by Dietrich Bonhoeffer." NPR. Macmillan Publishing Company. Accessed November 30, 2020. https://legacy.npr.org/programs/death/readings/spiritual/bonh.html.
27. Associated Press. "Slain Teacher's Kin Ask Forgiveness for Killers." *Chicago Tribune*, September 6, 1970.
28. "Forgiveness: Your Health Depends on It." Johns Hopkins Medicine. Accessed November 30, 2020. https://www.hopkinsmedicine.org/health/wellness-and-prevention/forgiveness-your-health-depends-on-it
29. Carfagna, Rosemarie. *Divine Designs: Exercises for Spiritual Growth*, 12. United States: Sheed & Ward, 1996.
30. Erb, Alta Mae. *Christian Nurture of Children*. Scottdale, PA: Herald Press, 1958.
31. Richards, Lawrence O. *365 Day Devotional Commentary*, 838. United States: Victor Books, 1990.
32. Lewis, Clive Staples. *Mere Christianity*, 104. United Kingdom: Macmillan, 1977.

33. Hemingway, Ernest. *The Old Man and The Sea*, 12. N.p.: World Heritage Publishers Ltd, 2015.
34. Heschel, Abraham Joshua. *The Wisdom of Heschel*, 219. United States: Farrar, Straus and Giroux, 1986.
35. Finley, James. *Merton's Palace of Nowhere,* 117. United States: Ave Maria Press, 1978.
36. Kazantzakis, Nikos. *The Last Temptation of Christ*, 5. United States: Simon & Schuster, 2012.
37. Lyon, Bill. "Cappelletti's high honor Joey's proudest moment." *Philadelphia Inquirer*, Dec. 14, 1973.
38. Ibid.
39. Ibid.
40. "Hilaritas." NumisWiki - The Collaborative Numismatics Project - Thousands Of Online Numismatic Books, Articles And Pages. Forum Ancient Coins. Accessed November 30, 2020. https://www.forumancientcoins.com/numiswiki/view.asp?key=hilaritas.
41. James, William. "The Religion of Healthy-Mindedness." *The Varieties of Religious Experience: A Study in Human Nature. Being the Gifford Lectures on Natural Religion, Delivered at Edinburgh in 1901-1902.* (1902).
42. "30 March 2013: Easter Vigil: Homily of Pope Francis." La Santa Sede, March 29, 2013. http://www.vatican.va/content/francesco/en/homilies/2013/documents/papa-francesco_20130330_veglia-pasquale.html.
43. Lonergan, Bernard J. F.., Doran, Robert M.., Crowe, Frederick E. *Collected Works of Bernard Lonergan: Collection*, 230-31. Canada: University of Toronto Press, 1988.
44. Merton, Thomas. *Thoughts in Solitude*, 99. New York: Farrar, Straus, Giroux, 2000.

WORKS CITED

45. Hillesum, Etty. *An Interrupted Life: the Diaries, 1941-1943; and, Letters from Westerbork*, 358-59. New York: Henry Holt, 1996.
46. "The Child by the Seaside: a Medieval Story about Saint Augustine." Medievalists.net, February 6, 2019. https://www.medievalists.net/2019/02/the-child-by-the-seaside-a-medieval-story-about-saint-augustine/.
47. Carretto, Carlo. *Letters from the Desert,* 12. United States: Orbis Books, 1982.
48. Solzhenitsyn, Aleksandr Isaevich. *The Gulag Archipelago, 1918-1956: An Experiment in Literary Investigation*, 615. United Kingdom: Harper & Row, 1975.
49. Steindl-Rast, David. *David Steindl-Rast: Essential Writings*. United States: Orbis Books, 2010.
50. Lonergan, Bernard J. F., Robert M. Doran, and John D. Dadosky. *Method in Theology*, 290. Toronto: Published for Lonergan Research Institute of Regis College, Toronto, by University of Toronto Press, 2017.
51. *The Holy Bible: Revised Standard Version*. New York: Thomas Nelson & Sons, 1952.

www.ingramcontent.com/pod-product-compliance
Lightning Source LLC
Chambersburg PA
CBHW072159100526
44589CB00015B/2287